ASK SUZE

. . . ABOUT MUTUAL FUNDS AND ANNUITIES

Riverhead Books
a member of
Penguin Putnam Inc.
New York
2000

ALSO BY SUZE ORMAN

You've Earned It, Don't Lose It

The 9 Steps to Financial Freedom

The Courage to Be Rich

ASK SUZE

...ABOUT MUTUAL FUNDS AND ANNUITIES

SUZE ORMAN

This publication is designed to provide accurate and authoritative information in regard to the subject matter covered. It is published with the understanding that the publisher and author are not engaged in rendering legal, accounting, or other professional service. If legal advice or other professional advice, including financial, is required, the services of a competent professional person should be sought.

Penguin Putnam Inc. and Riverhead Books are not affiliated or connected in anyway with *The "Ask Suze" Financial E-Newsletter* or any of the information contained therein.

RIVERHEAD BOOKS
a member of
Penguin Putnam Inc.
375 Hudson Street
New York, NY 10014

Published simultaneously in Canada

ISBN 1-57322-421-9
GEN-834

Printed in the United States of America
5 7 9 10 8 6 4

This book is printed on acid-free paper. ♾

Book design by Deborah Kerner and Claire Vaccaro

ACKNOWLEDGMENTS

I'd like to thank John Claghorn and Gus Ozag for lending their expertise to this book and Peter J. Smith for his help in compiling it.

ASK SUZE

. . . ABOUT MUTUAL FUNDS

AND ANNUITIES

Introduction

When you begin to learn about money, you also begin to learn about yourself. This may surprise you, since you have probably always considered these two notions—"me" and "my money"—to be as unalike as oil and vinegar. But they are much more connected than you think! After all, the "me" part of you decides how much risk you are willing to take with your money. The "me" part of you chooses to invest for either the short or the long term. The "me" part of you decides whether you will treat your money with respect or with indifference.

Money is only money. It has no human characteristics except the ones we give it. It has no emotions. You, on the other hand, are complicated and changeable, the sum of all your experiences and beliefs. You are not the same person today as you were twenty years ago, ten years ago, or even six months ago. But your money will take its cues from you and act in ways that you—and only you—decide, and for that reason among others, it is important to know yourself as well as possible.

In today's fast-paced society, it's hard to find or make the time to do your financial homework—the kind of background research that not only honors your money but allows it to reach its full potential. Picking and buying a stock is a lot like making a Chinese meal. Three-quarters of the time is spent in preparation, and one-quarter of the time—or less— is spent in the actual cooking. In the case of stocks, you should research the company whose stock you are interested in, read its annual report, and research its products and asset management. Then, finally, you can call your broker or go online to buy however many shares.

This is where mutual funds can come in handy. When you put money into a mutual fund, you are essentially hiring a trained professional to do the stock-picking for you. The fund manager is trained to locate the best-performing stocks of the type that you are looking for and buy them for the mutual fund. And there are a lot of mutual funds in existence these days—around 9,000, by some estimates. There are mutual funds for people interested in investing in small companies. There are mutual funds for people interested in investing in big companies. There are mutual funds for people interested in investing in a particular foreign country. There are mutual funds for people interested in investing in environmentally sensitive companies. The list goes on and on.

Another kind of investment that has gotten a lot of attention recently is known as an annuity. Annuities are one area of investing in which I see more misguidance than almost any other. If you are invested in an annuity, if you are about to invest in an annuity—even if you are not invested in an annuity—you must read this section, for sooner or later someone will try to convince you that this form of investment should be a part of your financial life. It may be true, but most likely it is not. You will learn what you should know about annuities and how they really work in the second part of this book.

Learning about money is, in many ways, learning about ourselves. You will find as you make decisions about money that you are discovering and coming to terms with lots of unexpected information about yourself. So read the following pages, and as you do, start asking yourself questions. By the end, I suspect you will probably know yourself and your money better than you did before you started.

Mutual Fund Basics

I've heard the term "mutual funds" for years, but I've never known what they are. What is a mutual fund?

A mutual fund is a kind of investment. It is essentially a pool, or a fund of money, that many investors have put their money into together—mutually—and toward the same goal. What is that goal? The answer depends on the particular mutual fund. There are many different mutual funds, with many different investment objectives. For example, one fund might concentrate on aggressive growth, and another may try to generate income. Every mutual fund has a clearly defined investment objective as well as guidelines determining how the fund's money may be invested.

Who decides how to invest all this money, and what do they invest it in?

All managed mutual funds are run by a fund manager, or a portfolio manager. The fund manager decides—according to the goal and the guidelines of his or her particular mutual fund—which individual stocks and/or bonds he or she thinks will outperform the market and give investors the greatest return on their money. The fund manager decides which stocks and/or bonds to buy, and when, and also decides if and when they should be sold. Sometimes these decisions are made by a team of people, but usually just one or two people decide, based on their judgment and on financial experts' research. A fund manager can make or break a fund, since he or she makes all the critical investment decisions regarding it.

What exactly am I buying when I buy a mutual fund?
You are buying actual shares in that particular mutual fund. A share represents a unit of ownership in the mutual fund, just as a share of stock in a publicly traded company represents your partial ownership of that company.

Why would I buy a mutual fund instead of buying individual stocks?
Many people buy shares of mutual funds for two reasons: They are just starting out in the investment world and they do not have a lot of money to invest, and they want to diversify their investments as much as possible. Let's say that you have $1,000 to invest. If you invest in a mutual fund, you are buying a small slice of a very big pie that contains a lot of different stocks and/or bonds. If something happens to one of the stocks in the mutual fund that you bought into—let's imagine that it went belly-up—you would not have lost all your money. Yes, your mutual fund may have gone down a little in value, but it wouldn't be a financial wipeout for you. Now, if you had invested the entire $1,000 in just one stock, and that stock went belly-up, well then, poof! There goes all your money! Why? Because you did not diversify. Intelligent diversification—that is, spreading your money out among a variety of different kinds of investments—is the key to being a smart investor. Thus, for smaller amounts of money, a mutual fund is a great way to achieve diversification.

So I don't need a lot of money to invest in a mutual fund. What is the minimum amount I need to get started?

Most funds require an initial investment of $500 to $1,000 if you are investing in an individual retirement account (IRA) and $2,500 to $3,000 outside of a retirement account. Vanguard, for instance, has a minimum of $3,000 if you open a regular account with them. But if you open an IRA at Vanguard, the minimum drops to $500. Most mutual funds work more or less the same way, although a few good ones will let you invest with minimums as small as $50 to $100. These include T. Rowe Price, (800) 638-5660; Fremont Funds, (800) 548-4539; Strong Funds, (800) 368-1030; Neuberger & Berman, (800) 877-9700; and TIAA, (800) 223-1200.

Are you saying that only people with small sums of money buy mutual funds?

Absolutely not! People with large sums of money buy into mutual funds, too, because they like the fact that a qualified financial expert is making the decisions about what and when to buy and sell. For these investors, the only decision to be made is which mutual fund to buy. Remember, once you have purchased a mutual fund, the only other decision you will have to make with your investment is when to sell it. From the point of buying to the point of selling, your money is in the hands of the portfolio manager.

Are all mutual funds diversified among hundreds of stocks?

No. Some mutual funds are diversified among hundreds, even thousands of stocks while some own only 20 or 30. A so-called "diversified" mutual fund is required to invest in at least 16 companies. The Securities and Exchange Commission (SEC) has tacked on another regulation: The assets of a mutual fund cannot be held in any more than 25 percent of any one company. In short, every mutual fund has the right to invest in different things. But in most cases, one of the characteristics of mutual funds is their amazing diversity. Not only do mutual funds offer you diversification in the stocks and bonds that make up the mutual fund, but mutual funds themselves have different goals, which offers another type of diversification.

Different Types of Mutual Funds

Growth Funds

Growth funds are geared toward making your money grow and therefore they do not invest primarily in stocks that generate a dividend—that is, a sum of money paid to shareholders out of earnings. If growth of your money is your objective, then these kinds of funds can prove to be financially very beneficial and lucrative in the long term.

An aggressive growth fund is aggressive in its investment philosophy, and therefore tends to be made up of stocks that are more speculative in nature and that tend to move faster up and down than the overall market. An aggressive growth fund may avoid investing in conventional blue-chip stocks, instead concentrating on less well-known securities in an attempt to make larger profits when and if the stock does take off. Keep in mind, the higher the rate of return you seek, the higher the risk. Please note that this is probably *not* the best fund for people whose objective is to keep their money safe and secure in the short term.

Income Funds

Income funds pay the investor dividends and/or interest, typically on a monthly basis. Income funds commonly invest in bonds, and accordingly, they are not as likely as growth funds to make you a lot of money. Instead, they tend to generate good, semi-predictable income. Income funds are popular with retirees who have seen their money grow during their working years and now want a monthly income that they can count on. To investors in income funds, regular income is more important than the growth or possible loss of principal.

Are there any downsides to investing in an income fund?

With income funds there is not much risk in a stable interest rate environment, and thus the returns on your investment are generally lower overall than those on a growth fund. Most investors who want income, however, are willing to accept this. What investors may not know is that with income funds, the price of shares tends to go down as interest rates go up, and up as interest rates go down. So if interest rates started to take off, it is probable you would not get your original investment back, or at least not for a long time.

Growth and Income Funds

Is there a way to combine growth and income in the same mutual fund?

Fortunately, there is a way. Growth and income funds tend to concentrate on growth first, then on income. There are also equity income funds, which do just the reverse. These funds concentrate on generating income first, then on getting you growth.

Balanced Funds

A balanced fund is a marriage of a fund that deals exclusively in stocks and one that deals exclusively with bonds (we will discuss bond funds later). It mixes the two, usually fifty-fifty. Balanced funds are less risky than plain old stock funds, but can be a little more precarious than bond funds in a bear (down) market.

International Funds

An international fund is a mutual fund that invests in stocks and/or bonds from foreign markets. Some of these funds invest in a single part of the world, such as Eastern Europe, and others put all their investments in a single country, such as Germany.

What is the difference between an international fund and a global fund?

International funds invest only abroad, whereas global funds invest in stocks and bonds in both the United States and abroad.

International funds seem risky, given the volatile state of the world today. Are they?

Again, risk is a relative term! If your mutual fund invests in several countries and not just one section of the world, this of course minimizes the risk to you, the shareholder.

There is a theory that the more countries or different financial markets an international mutual fund invests in, the less risk it presents to investors. This is because you are dealing with a great many different country-specific markets which don't always behave the same. For example, if one market in

Europe falls, another market in Asia may rise—sometimes in reaction to that falling European market. If your fund invests in one country, say, Hungary, the chances for a total loss—or, for that matter, an enormous gain—are greater. Remember, for most of us, diversification, whether we are investing here in the United States or abroad or both, is always important.

What is an emerging market fund?

An emerging market fund is a mutual fund that invests in a developing region of the world, whether it's the Far East or Eastern Europe. These funds generally concentrate on stocks that are inexpensive either in relation to their markets, or to the stocks of other, comparable companies in similar countries. They can be extremely volatile. Remember the meltdown in Southeast Asian markets and Brazil's recent financial woes? These are some of the potential hazards for the investor in an emerging market fund, but there are also some extraordinary bargains to be had in these funds, too.

I've heard talk about "sector funds." What does this term mean?

A sector fund is also known as a specialty fund. These are mutual funds that invest in the stocks of one particular kind of industry, whether it's telecommunications, utilities, chemicals, gold and precious metals, or pharmaceuticals. Some specialty funds are a lot riskier than others, but it depends on the fund's investments.

What is a socially responsible fund?

Typically, these funds follow strict guidelines as to what they can and cannot invest in, with the goal being to avoid companies that may cause harm to people, animals, or the environment. Most socially responsible mutual funds do not invest in tobacco or nuclear energy companies. Nor do they buy companies that have a history of discriminating against women or minorities, or of mistreating their employees, or companies that in any way have a history of harming the environment. You can find a comprehensive listing of socially responsible funds on the Internet, at *www.socialinvest.org*. My favorite is the Domini Social Equity Fund.

Large-cap, Mid-cap, and Small-cap

What is the difference between a company that is described as large-cap, one that is described as mid-cap, and one that is described as small-cap?

These designations refer to companies of a certain size, the "cap" here being shorthand for "capital." Small-cap generally refers to a corporation whose capitalization or market value falls below $1.5 billion. Mid-cap refers to companies whose capitalization runs between $1.5 billion and $5 billion. Large-cap companies have capitalization of $5 billion or more. There is a category below small-cap that you hear about less often, and that is "micro-cap," which is made up of companies with capitalization of less than 1.5 billion.

What is the difference between a large-cap growth fund, a large-cap value fund, and a large-cap blend fund?

A large-cap growth fund concentrates its investments in well-known, well-managed companies with proven track records and a history of outperforming the markets. There are relatively small dividends, if any, paid out, because you invest in this type of fund for long-term growth. A large-cap value fund, on the other hand, generally focuses its investments on companies that the fund manager believes are undervalued in price and that the rest of the investing world will someday recognize as the winners they are! A large-cap blend fund combines these two financial philosophies, and contains both growth stocks and value stocks.

Mid-cap and small-cap companies also use these classifications. A small-cap growth mutual fund will invest in new or smaller (generally, both) companies that are growing at an extremely rapid pace, and that are typically focused on some up-to-the-minute industry, such as computer technology. In general, fund managers purchase these shares early in the game and hold on to them for a long time. A small-cap value fund will concentrate its investments on better-established, though under-recognized, small companies. A "blend" of mid-cap or small-cap funds refers to a combination of these two investment styles.

Open- and Closed-end Funds

What is an open-end fund?

Most mutual funds are open-end funds. This means that there is no limit on the number of shares that the fund can issue or sell. This allows a fund to have as many investors as it wants, so the growth of the fund in terms of investment dollars is open-ended. An open-end fund's price is quoted as a net asset value, a NAV, rather than a price per share.

So you are saying that there is no set limit to the amount of money investors can put into an open-end mutual fund?

Correct. But the fund managers may sometimes close the fund to new investors once they've taken in more money than they feel is manageable. (Old investors usually can continue to put money into the fund.) This is a decision they can make at any time.

What's a closed-end fund?
A closed-end mutual fund is one in which the number of shares that can be sold to the public is established at the outset. New investors can buy into a closed-end fund only if someone who owns shares wants to sell them. A closed-end fund is essentially priced and traded just like a stock and is usually sold on the American Stock Exchange.

Closed-end funds are far less common than open-end funds. Open-end funds are the ones you usually hear people talking about, and are the ones commonly offered in 401(k) and 403(b) retirement plans.

Managed Mutual Funds and Indexed Mutual Funds

I've heard a lot lately on managed funds versus indexed ones. What is the difference between the two?
Managed mutual funds are run by a manager or a team of managers who decide what to buy and sell with the money the investors have deposited into the fund. An index fund also has a portfolio manager, but that manager simply buys the entire index that the fund is duplicating, such as the Standard & Poor's 500 Index.

What do fund managers look for when they are considering investing in a particular company?
Successful stock-picking is a mixture of intuition and knowledge informed by research, so fund managers usually track the market in a number of ways, which include scrutinizing price trends. For example, has the company in question shown a decent upward price trend? What about the industry involved? Is the U.S. economy in recession, or have interest rates declined?

Either situation can influence which kinds of stock the fund manager elects to invest in.

Most fund managers do hands-on research, too, and they are typically advised by research analysts within their company. They want to discover the goals of the company whose stock they are thinking of buying. They ask questions like: Where is the company in terms of research and development? Is there a product in the pipeline that can't lose? Has the company been profitable for a number of years? If so, what are the factors that have contributed to its winning streak?

Does the manager of the mutual fund have to inform me whenever he buys or sells something? And do I have to pay a commission when he does?

If you had a financial adviser at a full-service brokerage firm like Merrill Lynch, he or she usually would have to consult you before making any transaction, and you would most likely have to pay a commission whenever you bought or sold anything. This is not the case in a mutual fund, where the manager has free rein over the money in the fund and you're not charged an *individual* commission when each transaction is made. Before you purchase shares of your fund, you will receive a prospectus and reports outlining the mutual fund's activities, but you're not notified day to day. By buying shares in the fund, you have made the decision to trust the fund manager.

Rule of thumb: Before you buy into a managed mutual fund, check how long the manager has been in charge. Is the current manager the one responsible for a fund's terrific track record, or has that person moved on, leaving someone new and relatively untested at the helm? It's the *manager's* track record you want to know, not the fund's, because the manager ultimately creates the fund's success.

INDEXES

What is an index?
An index is simply a statistical indicator of how a particular group of stock or bonds is performing. There are several indexes that track the values in the stock and bond markets. The Dow Jones Industrial Average, for example, is an index based on 30 stocks. If these 30 stocks happen to go up overall, so does the Dow Jones index.

How many indexes are there in the United States?
There are a good number of them. Below, you will find a list of indexes, and the number of stocks or bonds that each of them tracks:

Wilshire 5000	7,174
Wilshire 4500	6,687
NASDAQ Composite	3,897
DFA U.S. 6-10 Small Co.	3,534
Russell 3000	3,000
NYSE Composite	2,881
DFA U.S. 9-10 Small Co.	2,769
DFA U.S. 6-10 Value	2,056
Russell 2000	2,000
Russell 1000	1,000
S&P 500	500
S&P/BARRA SmallCap 600 Value	392
S&P/BARRA Value	378
DFA U.S. Large Value	237

S&P/BARRA SmallCap 600 Growth	208
S&P/BARRA Growth	122
NASDAQ 100	100
DJIA	30

Can you give me a brief explanation of the most popular indexes?

Dow Jones Industrial Average (DJIA)

The DJIA is the most widely known, widely quoted daily financial index in the world. But it's also somewhat misleading, since it tracks only 30 large-cap blue-chip stocks and because it's "price-weighted," which means that the highest-priced securities in the index exert a disproportionate influence on how the DJIA does in general.

Standard & Poor's Composite Index of 500 Stocks (S&P 500)

The S&P 500 selects and tracks the 500 largely industrial stocks that appear in its daily index on the basis of their trustworthiness, liquidity, and group representation. Almost as widely quoted as the DJIA, the S&P 500 differs not only by the number of representative stocks it tracks but by its calculations, which, unlike the Dow's, are "market-weighted." This means that each stock's influence in the index mirrors its market value (the price of the stock multiplied by the number of outstanding shares).

Wilshire 5000 Equity Index

The Wilshire 5000 Equity Index follows the returns of practically every U.S. stock out there, though its name is slightly misleading, since nowadays it comprises about 7,000 different stocks.

Wilshire 4500 Equity Index

Take the Wilshire 5000 Equity Index, subtract the 500 companies that appear on the S&P 500 index, and you will have the Wilshire 4500 Equity Index. Like the Wilshire 5000, this index contains a far greater number of stocks than its name suggests.

Russell 3000

The Russell Index, which, like the S&P 500, is market-weighted, tracks the performance of some 3,000 large-cap U.S. companies representing nearly 100 percent of the U.S. equity market that is capable of being invested.

Russell 2000

This index takes the 2,000 smallest stocks on the Russell 3000 and gives them an index of their own. (Remember, "smallest" here is a relative term, given the size and stability of the securities tracked by the bigger Russell 3000.)

Schwab 1000

This market-weighted index comprises the 1,000 biggest publicly traded securities in America, including General Electric, Microsoft, Intel, Exxon, and Wal-Mart stores.

S&P MidCap 400 Index

Like the S&P 500, the S&P MidCap 400 Index is market-weighted and made up of stable, liquid companies with strong industry representation. Unlike the S&P 500, this index comprises 400 mid-cap securities.

S&P SmallCap 600 Index

The market-weighted S&P SmallCap 600 Index is made up of 600 small-cap stocks, again selected for their stability, liquidity, and industry representation.

Morgan Stanley Capital International Europe, Australia, Far East Index (MSCI EAFE)

This index is made up of roughly 1,000 stocks traded on some 21 different exchanges from Europe to Asia-Pacific.

Lehman Brothers Aggregate Bond Index (LB Aggregate Bond)

You didn't think that bond funds wouldn't have their own index, did you? The LB Aggregate Bond Index is made up of over 5,000 taxable government, corporate, and mortgage-insured securities. Its sheer size and complexity obliges most market analysts to take its daily measure through a sample.

American Gas Association Stock Index

This index tracks both producers and distributors of natural gas.

NASDAQ

NASDAQ stands for the National Association of Securities Dealers Automatic Quotations, also known as the over-the-counter market. The NASDAQ has no actual location but is instead a highly sophisticated computer system. This index tracks approximately 4,000 mostly technology-oriented stocks and is market-weighted, so that the largest stocks have more impact on the index level than smaller ones.

What is the best index to use if I am invested in large-cap growth funds here in the United States?

Besides the Dow Jones Industrial Average, the best index to track a growth mutual fund is the Standard & Poor's Index, the S&P 500. This index tracks 500 stocks of good-sized companies that are traded on the New York Stock Exchange. You will often hear this index quoted right alongside the Dow Jones.

Why do so many people buy index funds?

Over many years, index funds have outperformed almost 85 percent of all managed mutual funds. In the past few years, people have been making the greatest returns through investing in the S&P index funds. For many people, an index fund is an easy, hands-free way to invest. Their index fund simply buys all the stocks in the index they're interested in, and they do not have to worry about the fund's manager. In fact, one key to the better-than-average return on index funds is the exceptionally low cost of running them.

I have heard that there is a way to invest in the S&P 500 Index other than by buying an index fund. Do you know what that is?

You can invest in the S&P 500 Index by buying what is known as a SPDR, or "spider."

Standard & Poor's Depositary Receipts (SPDRs)

What is a SPDR?

Standard & Poor's Depositary Receipts, or "spiders," combine the features of an index fund with a stock. Like index funds, the SPDR trust portfolio is passively managed. Therefore, a SPDR is normally fully invested and does not attempt to time the market. SPDRs offer a level of diversification that would be difficult for you to achieve on your own or through outright ownership of the stocks. SPDRs and index funds are intended to track the price performance and dividend yield of the S&P 500 Index. As a result, the performance of these investments can be expected to move up or down in value with the S&P 500 Index.

What exactly am I buying when I buy a SPDR? Am I buying a stock or a mutual fund?

When you buy SPDRs you are buying units in a trust holding the S&P 500 stocks in proportion to their index weighting. The portfolio of S&P 500 securities held by the trust is adjusted as necessary to track changes made to the S&P 500 Index from time to time by Standard & Poor's. So in reality it is not a mutual fund although it acts almost the same as the S&P 500 index fund, since you are buying the entire index. It trades and behaves like a stock: There are no end-of-the-year distributions; you can buy and sell your shares during regular market hours; and there is no minimum investment amount as there is in many mutual funds.

Do SPDRs have a maturity date like a bond?

Technically, yes, although that date is more than 100 years in the future, and most likely will not affect you.

Do SPDRs pay a dividend?

The units provide quarterly cash dividend distributions based on the accumulated dividends paid by the stocks held in the SPDR trust minus an annual fee of 0.19 percent of principal to cover trust expenses. But please note the dividend is very, very low so do not count on this for income. This investment is for growth and growth alone.

How can I buy a SPDR?

SPDRs are traded on the American Stock Exchange under the symbol SPY. They can be bought or sold via a broker or on line throughout the trading day in the same manner as common stocks. The shares trade in 1⁄64 minimum increments and, as with regular stocks, there is a typical spread between the bid (what buyers are willing to pay) and asked price (what the sellers are asking for).

Am I better off buying a SPDR or a managed mutual fund?

That depends on which managed mutual fund you want to buy. In general, SPDRs have very low management fees and minimal security turnover, so in the past they have outperformed many actively managed equity funds. Remember, however, that historically, index funds also have outperformed the majority of actively managed mutual funds.

Am I better off buying an index fund or a SPDR?

That will also depend on how much money you have to invest and if you are investing inside or outside of a retirement account, as well as how often you expect to invest. Many of the good S&P 500 index funds require a high initial deposit ($3,000) to open an account. This is not true of a SPDR. If you want, you can buy one share, which could cost you as little as $100. Also, outside of a retirement account, SPDRs do have an advantage, tax-wise, over index funds. This is that the SPDR buys and sells shares only to adjust to changes in the composition of the S&P 500 Index. In SPDRs, there usually is not an end-of-the-year capital gain distribution as in mutual funds. Please note: Even index funds can have an end-of-the-year capital gain distribution.

If you plan to invest a small sum of money each and every month, you most likely will be better off in a no-load index fund, for if you invest directly there will be no transaction costs. If you buy SPDRs every month, even at just $8 a trade (remember, you have to pay a commission every time you buy or sell SPDRs), it will invariably cut into your profits.

One last thing to note. The expenses for SPDRs are somewhat less than the expenses of many index funds.

Are SPDRs easier to buy and sell than index funds?

Overall, they are. SPDRs are traded in the same manner as stocks, so you can get price quotes and make trades anytime during the day. You can also designate the exact price that you are willing to pay (limit order). One the other hand, the net asset value (the equivalent of share price) of a mutual fund is calculated only once per day, so if you want to purchase a mutual fund you will get the price of the shares at the closing price on the day your order is placed. The ability to buy or sell SPDRs anytime during the market day and to use any type of stock order gives you a wide range of opportunities to reduce your transaction costs and/or to implement market timing strategies. This characteristic can be particularly important during a large one-day decline in the stock market, since SPDRs enable you to liquidate your position during the course of the day rather than at the close of trading.

In a bear market, which is better to have, an index fund or a SPDR?

SPDRs can be more useful than index funds for timing the market. An investor who practices market timing can employ certain stock market strategies, which can't be done with index funds, such as a technique known as selling short. (I explain this strategy in *Ask Suze . . . About Stocks and Bonds.*) SPDRs are exempt from the uptick rule that requires shares to be sold short only at a price higher than the previous sale. Thus, SPDRs can be shorted on a downtick, which is very important during the major selloffs that characterize bear markets. Since research has indicated that about 90 percent of stocks will decline in value during a bear market, shorting a basket of stocks would appear to be a useful strategy during a market downturn. You cannot do this with an index mutual fund.

Are there other indexes or unit trusts that trade like SPDRs?

Yes. Over the years since their inception, the concept of SPDRs has caught on among investors. Now you can invest, for example, in SPDRs that track the Standard & Poor's MidCap 400 Depository Receipts (the symbol is MDY), which are for investors seeking more rapid growth and who are also willing to accept greater volatility. Want to invest globally? A cousin to the SPDR, World Equity Benchmark Shares (symbol WEBS), will weave investors into 17 selected major international equity markets. You can invest in the Dow Jones Industrial Average by buying DIAMONDS (symbol DIA). Want to buy an index which tracks 100 technology stocks like Microsoft,

Cisco, Intel, etc.? You can do that through the NASDAQ 100 (symbol QQQ). There are even nine individual Select Sector SPDR Funds that can give you ownership in a particular sector or groups of industries that are represented by a specified Select Sector Index. The nine Select Sector Indexes upon which the Select Sector SPDR funds are based together comprise all the companies included in the benchmark S&P 500. So as you can see, unit trusts are growing and growing, and are something that you need to know about.

There are so many mutual funds and unit trusts to choose from! How do I know which one is best for me?
The answer to this depends on your investment objectives and what you want out of your investments. Read on.

INVESTMENT OBJECTIVES

What I want out of my investment—what does that mean exactly?
This means that you know what you want from your money. Are you after long-term growth? Do you want regular income? Do you want a combination of long-term growth and income? When exactly will you need this money? Twenty years from now? Thirty years from now? Are you trying to put away money for your children's college educations? Are you looking for a fund that takes big risks for the possibility of even greater gains? How old are you? Are you a retiree who doesn't want to take any risks, or are you a 25-year-old daredevil with money and energy to burn? Investment objectives are a lot different for a 20-year-old than they are for a 63-year-old.

If you want your money to outpace taxes and inflation, you

must invest for growth. This means taking an active role in your future—and the future of your loved ones. Maybe the thought of investing all your money in one or two or three particular stocks frightens you. I don't blame you. But in mutual funds, your money is spread out among a variety of different stocks. So the chances are that if one of the stocks you have invested in starts to lose money, the other stocks will stay the same, or maybe even rise, which can stabilize your potential losses.

Is there an ideal time frame to consider when I begin investing?

It doesn't matter if you have a large lump sum you want to invest or if you're starting from scratch and want to put in a little here, a little there, when you can. Rule number one of investing for growth is that to invest wisely in the stock market, either with individual stocks or through mutual funds, you must invest only money that you will not need to touch for at least 10 years. Is that clear? If you are willing to commit your money for the long term, you are much more likely to see a return—a greater return—on your investment.

MUTUAL FUNDS

What if I decide I want to take some or all of my money out of the mutual fund? Am I allowed to?

Of course you are. It's your money. But remember, depending on the kind of mutual fund you purchased as well as the current price per share, you might end up taking out less than you put in. If you still want to take your money out, most mutual fund companies or brokerage firms offer investors an 800 number they can call to liquidate shares. Alternately, you can do it on line.

I am afraid that the market may go down after I invest in it, and I'll lose a lot of money. What can I do to limit my exposure?

You can use a technique I love called dollar cost averaging. Dollar cost averaging is an investment practice whereby you invest an unchanging dollar amount at regular intervals of your choice (preferably every month) into a specific investment vehicle. This method puts time, your money, and the market all on your side, regardless of what the stock market does over the short term.

Why should I spread my investment over time? Why don't I just wait and put all my money in when the market is at a low point?

What you are suggesting is called timing the market: buying low and selling high. Some people think they can time the market, but many have lost a lot of money trying to outguess it. If you wait till the market goes down to invest, chances are it will go up instead and you will have missed your moment. Or maybe you'll catch the market when it's down—but not as far as it's going to be next month.

You can find a lengthier discussion of the concept of dollar cost averaging in *Ask Suze . . . About Stocks and Bonds.*

What if there is an enormous stock market tumble and practically everything loses value? Will the diversification within my mutual fund protect me in this situation?

I'm glad you asked this. If the market as a whole loses a large percentage of its value, your mutual fund—despite its diversification—will probably lose money, too. In a bear market, where the majority of stocks tumble in value, diversifying your risk will probably not keep you from seeing the losses that everyone will experience. But this is where your commitment comes in, for if you are willing to weather the bear market, history has shown that the market will likely go up again and you will see positive returns.

Are there mutual funds that make money in a bear market?

Yes. As I said earlier, there are all kinds of mutual funds—including funds that invest in such a way that bear markets are advantageous to them. These kinds of funds are sometimes referred to as "foul weather" funds, or funds that have a strong performance in a bear market.

What are "fund families"?

"Fund family" is the cozy name given to a group of mutual funds that are managed by one particular investment company, such as Fidelity or Vanguard. While these mutual funds are under the same umbrella, they are all different from one another.

Some of the great fund families are:

Fidelity	(800) 544-9797
Invesco	(800) 525-8085
Janus	(800) 525-3713
T. Rowe Price	(800) 638-5660
Vanguard	(800) 622-7447

What to Look for When Picking a Mutual Fund

Are there any objective ways to determine which mutual fund is right for me?

First of all, you need to know your investment objective. After you have figured that out, you need to investigate the mutual fund's performance expense ratio, turnover ratio, sales charges, and policies, if any, on cash reserves, of the fund or funds that meet your objective. A good source of information is Morningstar (*www.morningstar.com*), a mutual fund rating service.

Okay, I've made a list of the things I need to know about a fund, but I have no idea what the terms mean and what I should be looking for.

Below are certain guidelines that you should use:

Expense Ratios

The manager of a mutual fund is paid by the fund's investors. The manager's salary is a percentage of the invested capital per year. In addition to paying the management fee, the investors also pay the fund's operating fees. Together, all these fees add up to what's called the *expense ratio* of the fund. Whatever the expense ratio is, it will definitely affect your rate of return.

I personally would never buy a fund with an expense ratio that is higher than 1 percent. Here's why: Let's say that during the course of one spectacular year, the manager of your mutual fund makes a return of 20 percent. Do you get that 20 percent? I wish I could tell you that you do, but before you get your money, the fund subtracts the expense ratio. If the expense ratio is 2.75 percent, your return will be 17.25 percent. So the expense ratio can affect your return significantly. And when you calculate the effect this high expense ratio has on the growth of your money over time, you will be amazed.

One of my favorite index funds has a total expense ratio of 0.20 percent, and it does really well. Why in the world would you want to pay someone to manage your money for you if that person couldn't consistently outperform the index that his or her fund is comparing its performance to? You wouldn't. One of the reasons managed funds don't perform as well as index funds is because of high expense ratios.

Turnover Rate

The turnover rate of a mutual fund refers to the cumulative dollar amount of common or preferred stock that the fund manager buys or sells in a given year. If you see that a particular mutual fund has a 100 percent turnover rate, this means that during the year in question, the fund manager "turned over" the entire amount of his or her portfolio.

What can I infer from a 100 percent turnover rate?

The higher the turnover rate, the more likely it is that you have a very aggressive fund manager who loves to buy and sell the stocks in the mutual fund often. Now, if you see that a mutual fund has a turnover rate of 25 percent, then you can infer from this that the fund manager has a more conservative philosophy when it comes to buying and selling the assets of the fund. Personally, I am always on the lookout for lower portfolio turnover rates—from 20 to 50 percent—especially if the money is outside of a retirement account. This is because the higher the turnover rate, the more capital gains taxes you may have to pay at year's end, and the more commissions the fund has to pay to cover all the trades.

So if you saw that a mutual fund had a 300 percent turnover rate, you consider this a bad sign?
No, not necessarily. But I still would feel most comfortable investing in a mutual fund with a lower turnover rate, say about 50 percent. Again, a portfolio with a high turnover rate may generate lots of year-end taxes (we will be discussing this later on), and if your money is not inside a retirement account, this could mean potential tax trouble for you.

Do index funds have a turnover rate?
Yes, but usually only about 5 percent a year. This is because the portfolio manager does not buy and sell stocks based on his own investment strategy. He only does so to match the index he is tracking.

Sales Load

A sales charge, or load, is basically the fee involved in buying or selling the fund. You should always look for a no-load fund. (I will discuss no-load funds later on—they are the only way to go in my opinion.)

Cash Reserve

A fund's cash reserve is the amount of actual cash kept by a fund to buy stocks or bonds. A fund's cash reserve is another indicator of how the portfolio manager feels about the stock market. If there's a large cash reserve, it suggests that the fund is not fully invested because its manager fears the market will go down and he or she doesn't want to risk exposure, or the manager wants to have available cash to buy stocks at a good price. On the other hand, if the cash reserve is low, then the fund is more fully invested, suggesting that the fund's manager is bullish and feels confident that the market is the best place to realize high returns. This rule is not universally applicable, however, since some funds have to stay 100 percent invested according to the terms of their prospectus.

In a bull market, I like funds that, like index funds, need to be totally, completely invested all the time. If a mutual fund keeps a large percentage of its money in cash, then the overall return will most likely not be as high. In my opinion, you should buy into a fully invested fund and be prepared to stay put.

Betas

What is the "beta" of a mutual fund?

You can figure out your mutual fund's volatility—how much the share price or NAV goes up and down—in a couple of ways. One of these ways is by looking at the fund's beta, which basically is a measurement of the riskiness of your mutual fund in comparison to the overall market. A mutual fund with a beta of 1 is projected to move in direct correlation to the stock market. If the market goes up or down 10 percent, the share price or NAV of this fund should also move up or down 10 percent. If the mutual fund you are considering has a beta greater than 1, then the fund will probably move faster—both up and down—than the overall market. The higher the beta, the more aggressive, and therefore the riskier, the fund.

What if my mutual fund has a beta less than 1?

Your mutual fund will be less volatile than the market. It may not dip as low as the market, but on the other hand, it probably won't match sharp market gains, either.

Moving Average

What do economists mean when they use the term "moving average"?

A moving average is a widely used and occasionally very accurate indicator of the way markets and funds are moving. It predicts future behavior by tracking the average of the stock market and the average share price of a mutual fund over a specific period of time. For instance, there is an average known as the 39-week (that's about 9½ months) moving average. The 39-week moving-average theory holds that if the average share price has gone up over that time frame then it will probably continue to go up. Conversely, if the average share price has dropped, it will probably continue to fall.

What's the use of a moving average?

For one thing, it tells investors whether or not the price of the mutual fund seems to be gaining on the market or whether it is on a steady downward curve. If the fund's trend is up over the moving average, it's probably a good time to buy. If its trend is downward, then you might want to sell. In other words, if the market overall is going up, and you picked a lemon of a fund that is not keeping up with the market averages, then you're better off getting out of that fund and into one that is performing. If the market is going down, and your fund is in line with what's happening, then you should probably hang in there. So in this sense, the moving average is one way to monitor whether you've chosen a good fund or a lemon.

How is the moving average of a mutual fund figured out?

Let's use the 39-week moving average as an example. The simple explanation is that economists take the average price of 39 weeks' worth of your fund's net asset value and see how the most recent price compares with the 39-week average. Remember, if the price of your fund is above the moving average, many professionals take this as a sign that you should continue to buy. If it is below the moving average, they take this as a sign that you should sell, and park your funds in a money market fund until you decide what to do with them in the long term.

Are moving averages a reliable way to make decisions about investing?

Moving averages are useful to know about because financial professionals use them when trying to assess the market. But in my opinion, a moving average should not make or break your decision to buy or sell shares of a mutual fund.

Fund Performance

Does the past performance of a mutual fund play an important role in making a decision to buy into it?

Not necessarily. A fund's performance history doesn't always tell you what will happen after you buy the fund. If a fund has done spectacularly well over a long period, its apparently great performance could have resulted simply from special circumstances—such as a fund manager's investing a large sum of money in one sector that's hot (think of Internet stocks in the late '90s)—and not from impressive overall returns. On the other hand, knowing a fund's past performance provides useful information—specifically, whether the fund is stable or not. By "stable," I mean: Does it stay in line with what the market does? Or does it wander all over the place, with no relation to the market at all? If you are buying a managed mutual fund, in particular, you should look for stability and a fund that outperforms the market index most closely related to it.

What does net asset value mean?

The net asset value, or NAV, is the share price of the fund. At the end of each day, the entire value of the portfolio of stocks and/or bonds, less any expenses and/or liabilities, is added up. That total is divided by the number of shares outstanding. This figure is called the net asset value, or NAV. It is what each of your shares is worth. If you are a new investor and want to invest $1,000 into this mutual fund, and the NAV on the day you purchased your fund was $10 a share, you would own 100 shares of the mutual fund.

What is the yield of a fund and how is it figured?

The yield is what a fund pays to investors in dividends over the course of a year. A fund's yield tells you the kind of income you can expect to receive from the fund, which you can either receive in cash payments or reinvest by purchasing additional shares of the mutual fund. So, for example, if the NAV of your mutual fund is $12, and your mutual fund pays $0.72 a year in dividends, then the yield is $0.72 divided by $12, or 6 percent.

What does the total return of a fund tell me?

The total return is a measure of the dividends paid by a fund as well as any realized and unrealized appreciation or depreciation of the fund's investments for a stated period. The total return is particularly important when it comes to bond funds. In a bond fund you can be getting a yield of 5 or 6 percent, but the price per share of the bond fund could have declined, so that the total return of the fund, taking into consideration the yield and the decline of the shares, could be a negative figure. In my opinion, the total return is the only figure that counts when analyzing a mutual fund's performance.

How much should I expect to make in a mutual fund?
Historically, funds that buy and sell common stocks have a return of around 10 percent annually, corporate and U.S. government bonds 5 percent, and T-bills less than that. But remember, these figures are averages. You could invest one year and lose 15 percent and the next year make 25 percent, which means your average yearly return would be 3.125 percent (because you'll earn the 25 percent on a smaller amount—since you lost 15 percent). Over time and with patience and a bull market, money is made.

Evaluating Risk

Would you caution me against anything as I begin to look for the mutual fund that's right for me?
I've said it before and I'll say it again: You should invest in mutual funds for the long haul. Please remember that mutual funds are long-term investments, and they must be treated as such. Therefore, you must take the time and make the effort to find the right mutual fund for you. Don't chase after the flavor-of-the-moment fund or the one that your cousin Ruby has given you a tip about. Don't invest in order to make a quick killing, because more often than not, you'll end up disappointed.

Are you telling me not to take any risks?
I am not saying that. A huge part of anybody's financial journey involves figuring out his or her own comfort level with risk. If you are an inexperienced or first-time investor, I would advise against taking outrageous risks, but I would also advise

against playing it too safe with a money market account or CDs. One way to guard against and balance potential losses is, again, to diversify. This simply means that you should consider investing in more than one mutual fund and should choose funds that don't duplicate each other. That way, if one of your funds makes a lot of money and another loses value, you stand a good chance of coming out even, if not ahead.

Is there a difference between the types of mutual funds that are best for me when I am young versus when I am middle-aged?

It is a fairly good rule of thumb that the younger you are, the more you can afford to take risks. If you are 20 years old, you probably don't have a spouse or children yet, and you also have time to rebuild any assets that you might lose. Thus, for the younger investor, who can afford to take on greater risk for the sake of maximum growth, I would advise aggressive growth funds. The older you get and the more financial responsibilities you assume, the more I recommend that you diversify. You can invest in stocks and bonds, and you can also open up a money market account. For most people who are nearing retirement age, income is the most important concern. At this point, more conservative investments—money markets, CDs, and bond funds, for example—probably make more sense for the majority of your portfolio. However, there is always room for at least 20 percent of your assets to be invested in the stock market regardless of your age.

The Prospectus

I think that I've found a mutual fund that feels right for me. Should I contact the company?
Yes, if only to talk to a customer service representative and have him or her send you a prospectus.

What is a prospectus?
A prospectus is a legal document that describes, usually in some detail, the investment goals of the mutual fund in question and the investment costs involved along the way. It also tells you who is in charge of the fund. It's easy to get hold of a prospectus, and in fact, federal law requires that you receive a prospectus before you are allowed to invest even one cent in any mutual fund. Call up the fund company and request one.

If you're unsure of a specific fund's name but are interested in, say, aggressive growth funds, the customer service representative will be able to send you information on various funds that meet your investment objective.

I've got my prospectus in hand, and I must say it's pretty intimidating. What am I looking at here?
A prospectus can be very intimidating at first glance, but don't let it scare you. Just look for the important facts that you want to know: the sales load, the objective of the fund, the fees and expenses, and the manager. And remember, you can always call the fund's 1-800 number to find out more information.

What is inside the prospectus?

A mutual fund's prospectus includes an explanation of the objectives of the fund; tables that compare the fund's performance over the past several years with that of various indices, such as the S&P 500; a brief analysis of the risks of investing in the fund; and a schedule of any fees that may be charged to investors. You can find out from the prospectus whether the mutual fund is a growth or an income fund. The prospectus will also tell you who manages the fund. Typically, you will *not* find a current listing of the securities that the mutual fund owns, mostly because they may change from one month to the next. You will find this information in the annual report, which is sent to the fund's investors once a year.

The prospectus in front of me says that the mutual fund is interested in "capital appreciation." What kind of mutual fund is this?

"Capital appreciation" is just an official-sounding way of saying that you are dealing with a growth fund.

A section in the prospectus explains the fund's various fees. What should I be on the lookout for?

You should check what the fund's management fees are (you usually want to see a number between 0.25 and 1 percent). You will also find a list of fees for various services, including how much it will cost you to have money wired or electronically transferred to your checking or savings account. Also check to see if the fund charges you for reinvesting dividends. And read the fine print for other minor operational expenses. Most important, you want to see if the fund is a load or a no-load fund. In my opinion, no-load funds are the way to go. Here's why.

Load Versus No-load

Over the years, mutual funds have become immensely popular, so it is important that you understand how they really work. When mutual funds first came on the scene, you could buy them only through a broker, and they were all loaded funds, which meant there was a sales charge on the initial purchase and every subsequent transaction. Then slowly but surely, a new breed of mutual funds known as no-load funds emerged. These funds did not have a sales charge on them. Investors soon recognized the value of no-load funds and started investing very heavily in them. This put a big dent in the profits of brokerage firms that sold only loaded funds, so they came up with another kind of fund—or, in my opinion, a way to make you think you could buy a no-load fund through them—a back-end load, or 12(b)1, fund.

Now there are many varieties of funds. The three most common are front-end load funds, no-load funds, and back-end load funds. As their names suggest, the load funds charge you a commission fee just for buying the fund. No-load funds carry no commission fee, although like all funds, they have some maintenance fees. Let's talk about front-end load funds first.

Front-End Load Funds, or A Shares

Front-end load funds are identified as A-share mutual funds. If the name of a mutual fund has an "A" or says "A shares" after it, then you know it's a front-end load fund. Front-end load funds charge a load, or a fee, up front. This is the commission that the broker or the financial planner takes before your money even gets invested. The commission can be anywhere from 2 percent to 8.5 percent; the average commission is about 5 percent—out of your pocket! Think of this load as an unnecessary burden on your money.

C Shares

Fund shares that are on a level-load basis are known as C shares. When you buy C shares, you are charged a level load, or an annual percentage, around 0.75 percent to 1 percent of the value of the account which is taken directly out of your fund's earnings each and every year. These funds are not as popular as A- or B-share load funds or no-load funds when it comes to fee structures.

No-load Funds

A no-load fund is a mutual fund that does not cost you a penny to buy or to sell. In other words, it does not have a load (commission). I believe no-load mutual funds are the only way to go. Look at it this way: If you were to invest $10,000 in a no-load mutual fund and decided, two days later, that you wanted to withdraw your money, you'd get all $10,000 back, assuming the market hadn't moved. If you invested $10,000 in a loaded fund and wanted your money back, you would get back only about $9,500. Think about that—a loaded fund has to go up approximately 5 percent just for you to break even. That means in a loaded fund you are starting out with a 5 percent disadvantage! That makes no sense.

Back-End Load Funds, or 12(b)1 Funds, or B Shares

In my opinion, B shares are the worst type of mutual funds you can buy. B shares are another type of loaded fund that locks you into a period of time—usually five to seven years—that you cannot sell the fund without being hit with a surrender charge. This fee usually starts at 5 percent the first year, dropping to 4 percent the second, 3 percent the third, 2 percent the fourth, 1 percent the fifth, and nothing thereafter.

My broker told me a B fund wouldn't cost me anything if I just stayed in there for 10 years. What's so bad about that?

I can't tell you how angry this makes me. What your broker fails to tell you is that you *are* paying to be in that fund whether you know it or not. You see, the broker who sold you the fund probably received a 5 percent commission, paid by either the firm he works for or the fund itself, up front and in full at the time you made the purchase. The way the brokerage firm or mutual fund company gets its money back is by charging you what is known as a 12(b)1 fee of anywhere from 0.75 to 1 percent yearly. This fee is taken out of the fund's returns. So if your fund earns 10 percent, and your 12(b)1 fee is 1 percent, your return is only 9 percent, because the brokerage firm or fund is taking that 1 percent to pay itself back for the commission it paid to the broker who sold you the fund. That is why your surrender charge goes down by that 1 percent each year. Suppose your fund paid a broker 5 percent up front and they take 1 percent a year from your return. If you were to sell after one year, your surrender charge would be 4 percent. Add that to the 1 percent they already took—and they've recouped the money they paid the broker. Pretty sneaky, don't you think?

Some B shares automatically convert to A shares after the surrender period, but some do not, and you continue to pay that 12(b)1 fee every year for as long as you own the fund—even though the broker has been paid! Again, in my opinion, B shares came about simply because brokerage firms needed to find a way to keep your business by luring you into a load fund under the guise of being a no-load fund.

Can you illustrate the effect of 12(b)1 fees with an example?

I sure can. Below are the actual returns of a growth fund from a major brokerage firm that has both A and B shares. Note the difference between the returns of the two. Remember that these are shares of the *same fund,* managed by the same portfolio manager. The only difference is that one set of returns is on the A shares and the other is on the B shares. I have chosen this fund because it is rated a four-star fund by Morningstar as of the writing of this book.

Annual Return Percentage	1997	1998
A Shares	28.70	33.49
B Shares	27.19	32.05
Difference	1.51	1.44

Trailing Return Percentage	1-Year Average	3-Year Average
A Shares	19.88	27.86
B Shares	18.54	26.45
Difference	1.34	1.41

Merrill Lynch Asset Gr Opp B
Merrill Lynch Asset Gr Opp A
(Source: *www.morningstar.com*, 7/31/99)

Take a good look and you will see the return on the A shares is more than 1 percent higher than the return on the B shares.

Why? Because of that 12(b)1 fee that you are paying out of your own pocket! If you look at the trailing return percentage, which is your average return if your money was in the mutual fund for all of one or three years, you will see that the 12(b)1 fee again makes more than a percent difference in your return. Remember, this is the same fund with the same holdings and the same manager. But B-share holders realize a lower return—because they are paying the fund out of their return!

Is the 12(b)1 charge in lieu of any other charges in my mutual fund?

Hardly. The 12(b)1 fee is in *addition* to all the other fees. You still have to pay the management fees and other expenses of the fund, just as you do with a no-load fund or an A-share fund. The 12(b)1 fees exist only to pay the broker's or financial adviser's commission.

Why would my financial adviser try to sell me these B shares of a fund?

Because that's how he or she makes a living. Please make sure to choose your financial adviser carefully—true financial advice means telling you, the client, how to get the most out of your money, even if it means the adviser won't make a lot of money from the transaction. Advisers are there to help you get rich, not to get rich off you. It's the adviser's responsibility to tell you if there's a less expensive way for you to make money—and to give you the choice of what you want to do after explaining how much each of your options will really cost you.

Does a loaded fund perform better than a no-load fund?

The answer is no. Many brokers or so-called financial advisers tell their clients that loaded funds do perform better, but that is not necessarily true. The person who sold you the fund has absolutely nothing to do with the performance of that fund. He or she is not the one who buys and sells the stocks or bonds. He or she simply sold you the fund, and for that you are paying him or her about 5 percent. You should think of him or her as you do a car salesman. When you buy a car, what does the person who sold you the car have to do with its performance? Nothing. That's right. The same is true of the person who sold you the mutual fund.

So what you're telling me is that if I am going to use a financial adviser to buy a fund, I'm better off buying A shares than B shares?
Yes. If, for whatever reason, you still want to use a financial adviser and buy a loaded mutual fund, you are better off buying A shares than B shares. If you do buy A shares, make sure you ask your broker about the breakpoint for the load on the fund you are thinking about buying.

What does the term "breakpoint" mean?
The breakpoint of a load fund is the amount of money you have to invest in that fund in order for you to get a reduced sales load. The amount depends on the mutual fund in question, but in general, the more money you invest, the lower the sales load will be. The first breakpoint level for many mutual funds is $25,000. Keep in mind that breakpoints apply only to loaded mutual funds. In a no-load fund, there is obviously no load from which you would need a break.

I have heard that investors can qualify for a breakpoint if they sign a "letter of intent." What is this?
A letter of intent (LOI) tells the mutual fund that you intend to invest an amount of money greater than or the same as one

of the fund's breakpoint levels (mutual funds often have more than one breakpoint level). If you write that letter, then you will not be charged the higher load.

How long do I have to invest this money?
Typically, 13 months.

What if the 13 months goes by and I haven't invested the entire amount?
An LOI isn't legally binding. But if you have not reached the investment level you stipulated in the LOI, you will be penalized by the fund for the difference between the lower load that you paid and the regular sales commission. Remember, you wouldn't have achieved your particular breakpoint—and thus a lower sales commission—without this LOI.

What is a "right of accumulation"?
For the investor who hasn't qualified for a breakpoint either through a larger investment or an LOI, a right of accumulation provides a lower load if the investor manages to reach a certain amount of money over several years' time (as opposed to 13 months). Although the lower load is not retroactive, the new, reduced load applies to all future purchases, as well as to the purchase that catapulted the investor over the breakpoint limit.

What is a redemption fee?
A redemption fee is a percentage the fund charges you to withdraw your money from that fund. This is different from a surrender fee, which usually goes away after a period of time. A redemption fee is in place for the life of the fund, and it usually runs about 1.5 percent. It is important that you know if your fund has a redemption fee or not.

Can a fund be a no-load fund and still have a redemption fee?

Yes. Remember, the load is what the broker who sold you the fund gets, and that is very different from a redemption fee. A redemption fee is what the fund company gets if you withdraw your money. So check it out. They are not that common, but they are out there.

My broker tells me that all mutual funds have loads on them. Is this true?

Well, it is true that all mutual funds have what are known as expense ratios, some higher than others. This expense ratio, a percentage of the total investment in the fund, pays the salary of the portfolio manager who is buying and selling the stocks and/or bonds, as well as expenses incurred in actually running the fund.

However, the actual sales load, which is what we are referring to here, is a whole separate issue. Not all funds have sales loads, and those that do are in my opinion a waste of your money. Remember, a sales load is what your broker gets to sell you the fund—the operative word is *sell*—to invest your money.

So you are telling me that the only way to go is through a no-load mutual fund?

That is exactly what I am saying. There are some 2,000 mutual funds out there that will charge you no commission whatsoever to invest with them. What's more, no-load funds can be purchased without the help of an adviser—no middleperson, no commissions, no hidden costs, just smooth sailing to greater and greater wealth over time.

How can I find a listing of all the no-load funds that are out there?
There is an organization known as the 100 Percent Mutual Fund Council, which every year puts out a listing of no-load mutual funds. A copy costs $5. You can write them at 1501 Broadway, Suite 1809, New York, NY 10036. Their phone number is (212) 768-2477, or you can access their website at *www.100noloadfunds.com.*

Can I save money by investing in mutual funds on line?
Not if you are buying a true no-load fund. A no-load fund will not cost you anything if you buy it directly through the company, so in this case online trading or purchasing will not save you money; it just might make it easier for you.

I want to buy a no-load fund via a discount brokerage firm, but they charge a fee. Is this a load?
No. This is what is known as a *transaction fee*. If you want to save yourself that transaction fee, you can do so by purchasing this fund directly through the fund family itself and not through that particular discount brokerage firm. There are discount brokers, however, that do not charge a transaction fee. It's worth your while to check around.

RATING MUTUAL FUNDS

When I read financial magazines, they each name a different mutual fund as the best fund of the year. How is that possible?
Great question—it is strange, isn't it? The answer is that each magazine uses different formulas and factors to calculate the

returns of the funds. They use different indexes to compare them, and they analyze the risk factors very differently. This is why they are all different.

Well, if they are all different, what factors should I use to rank the mutual funds that I want to buy?

Whenever you rank a mutual fund, consider its three- to five-year performance history. If the fund has had the same manager for the last few years, it's useful to see how he's done, if he has "what it takes." Now, as I've noted earlier, just because a fund's manager did well in the past is not a guarantee that he—or his fund—will continue to perform well in the future. However, past performance is one factor of several to consider and it is definitely something I would want to know before buying into a fund.

I would also go over the following checklist for every fund you evaluate:

- Always compare the fund you are about to buy with other funds that invest similarly. Remember, not all funds, even though they may be the same *kind* of fund, are alike.
- Take into consideration the risk of the fund. If the fund has had a great performance but the risk it had to take to get it was extremely high, then this fund may not be right for you. Always make sure you look at the risk of a fund and make sure that it meets your goals and comfort level.
- As I said earlier, get the prospectuses and annual reports of many mutual funds that are in the investment objective category that you are interested in and compare the funds' management, expenses, loads, fees, charges, distributions, tax implications, and services.

- Try to use the online services that rank the funds for you. The rating service Morningstar (*www.morningstar.com*) is my personal favorite.

I still don't feel that I have what it takes to pick my funds myself. Is there an unbiased resource that can help me?
One of my favorite resources is the *Bob Brinker Marketimer* newsletter, which you can get by calling (914) 591-2655 weekdays between 9 A.M. and 5 P.M. Eastern time. Bob is also on ABC radio for three hours every Saturday and Sunday. He's had his show for more than a decade, and gives terrific advice. He tells you which funds to buy and sell—and when. Tune in and start learning—and if you have a question, call it in. Bob also has a website at *www.bobbrinker.com.*

Keeping Tabs on Your Mutual Fund

After I buy a mutual fund, how can I keep track of its progress? Also, what if there is a change within the fund company—say, the manager of my fund leaves?
The easiest way to track your fund's progress is to check it in the business section of the newspaper. Or better yet, enter your holdings on the Internet in services such as Quicken.com or Yahoo!, or on AOL, to name a few. If you just enter the name of your fund, the date you bought it, the price you paid, and the number of shares you own, the service will automatically show you what your fund is worth every time you click on.

Some services will also alert you to any news you should be aware of concerning your fund.

Can you explain how I can find out how my fund is doing in the business section of the newspaper?
Yes, though please realize it may take some time for you to figure out how to interpret this information. Pick up a copy of the *New York Times* or the *Wall Street Journal* or, on the weekend, *Barron's,* and scan the part of the business section devoted to mutual funds. Find the name of your fund—say, Vanguard Total Stock Market Index. Next to it you will find the "buy" price of the fund. Next to the "buy" price will be the "sell" price, followed by the "change," or the amount the fund went up or down since the previous day. If the fund is a no-load fund, then the buy price and the sell price will be the same. If it is a loaded fund, then those two numbers will be different. Why? Because the sales load you pay to the broker is built into the price of the fund. "Return" refers to the total return of the fund. Depending on which newspaper you are reading, the return might indicate return for the year-to-date, or it might refer to a longer period (the newspaper will indicate the period of return).

How often should I check to see how my fund is doing?
You can check your funds as often as you like—it's your money, after all. Please remember, though, that mutual funds are long-term investments, and a fund that has dipped downward one day may surprise you a month later with an upward trend.

You mentioned Morningstar earlier. Are there other resources that will steer me toward, or away from, various mutual funds?

Yes. There is an enormous number of resources at your disposal, both on line and off. I have always been a big fan of the *Value Line Mutual Fund Survey*, a publication you can usually find in the reference section of your local library. Value Line lists approximately 2,000 funds, rated from one to five, one being the best and five the worst. Value Line also lists the annual rates of mutual funds over a number of years, making it easy for the investor to see how the fund has performed historically. But I would caution you against choosing a mutual fund solely on the basis of a good rating from Value Line or any other resource. Remember, past performance is not a guarantee of a fund's future performance, and ratings can change in the blink of an eye.

That said, you'll find a list of Internet resources at the back of this book.

In addition to considering my fund's past performance, are there any other ways to evaluate how it is doing?

A good way to evaluate your fund's performance is to compare it to the performance of other, comparable funds as well as to the index to which your fund is attached. Compare the average return of your fund with that of other funds and the index over the past few months, and over the past year. If your fund is totally underperforming, then you need to find out why and/or get into a new fund.

When to Buy and When to Sell

What if my mutual fund didn't outperform the S&P 500? Is that a sign that I should get rid of it?

No, not necessarily. In fact, it's surprisingly difficult in recent years for a managed fund to outperform an index. And even index funds will show lower returns than the index they track, simply because some fees must be deducted. Remember, you cannot just get out of a fund without thinking about the income-tax ramifications. But if the fund continues to significantly underperform the index *and* the tax consequences are not too high, then yes, I would switch.

The mutual fund that I invested in three years ago started off brilliantly, but it hasn't been doing so well recently. It had an excellent performance record when I bought it and now it seems to be sinking. What's going on?

Your mutual fund could be disappointing you for a number of reasons. If you invested in a growth fund, you may find yourself in a cycle where the securities typically chosen for such a fund are temporarily out of favor. Your fund manager may have made decisions or judgments based on speculation that never came to pass (remember, it is terribly difficult, if not impossible, to outwit the markets; there are too many factors at play!). Your fund manager might have bet that the stock market was poised for a fall and put a lot of the mutual fund's assets in cash as a hedge against a massive drop in stock prices, but instead, the market, against all odds, kept going up. Then again, your fund could be doing poorly because of instability abroad. Is there a war going on, or the threat of war in the wind? How are the foreign markets doing? Closer to home, what are interest rates doing? What is the unemployment rate? Did your fund manager buy small-cap stocks that may not have moved? There are many reasons a fund does not perform.

My mutual fund has just merged with another fund whose track record over the past few years has been iffy at best. Should I get out while the going is good?

This is a good question, because we have been talking about the performance of the markets, rather than about you, the investor. If for any reason you change your investment objectives, or if for any reason the infrastructure of the fund's management undergoes a change that you are not comfortable with, then by all means you should take this opportunity to sell your mutual fund, as long as you have considered the tax ramifications. Remember, it is your money, and you are in charge of putting it to work in a way that makes you feel the most comfortable.

For what reason would somebody change their investment objectives?

Investors change their financial objectives all the time and for all sorts of reasons. Say you get older and decide that you want to start getting dividends. Or, what if your spouse suddenly gets ill, and you know that you might have a lot of previously unexpected medical expenses in the next year? In this case, you may not be comfortable keeping your money in that growth-oriented mutual fund. You might be more comfortable putting most of your money in a money market fund.

As you get older, from time to time you will want to rethink your investment objectives. If your objectives and the fund's objectives are not a perfect or near-perfect match, this is the time to sell your fund.

Is there a relationship between how well the economy is doing and how well—or how poorly—a particular kind of mutual fund does?

That's a very good question, and the answer, typically, is yes. Let's take sector funds as an example. Remember that with a sector fund, you are taking a gamble on a particular industry, whether it's chemicals, or pharmaceuticals, or medical supplies. What happens when the economy starts to take off? The securities of industries involved in manufacturing, such as heavy metals and chemicals, tend to swing upward, anticipating work and demand. What happens when the economy starts to slow down? Well, in this circumstance, the general emphasis is on slower and steadier industries, such as health care and consumer goods.

What economic signs are important in determining the market's long-term movement, which obviously will affect growth mutual funds?

There are many financial signs that I think are important to watch, but the ones that have the biggest impact, in my opinion, on the stock market in general—and that are easy for you to monitor—are the following:

- Economic growth
- Interest rates
- Inflation
- Price of the dollar

What am I looking for in these different areas?

Well, the stock market is like a pot of soup: For good results, all the ingredients have to be just so. In my opinion, for a truly strong market you need:

- Slow economic growth
- A strong dollar overseas
- Reduced inflationary expectations
- Low interest rates

Do all four of these things matter?

Yes, because they all work off one another. If you have a weak dollar overseas, interest rates tend to rise here in the United States. But with rising interest rates comes fear of inflation, which is the stock market's biggest enemy. Do you see how a change in one factor can set off a chain reaction?

A market that is starting to weaken, and one that you have to watch very carefully, is one that has strong economic growth, rising short-term interest rates, increased inflationary expectations, and a weak dollar.

Now you see how important it is to follow our economy. Understanding how it works will help you make informed decisions about your investments. Remember, investing in mutual funds is a delicate balance—you have to know if and when you should sell, or buy, or just shift the balance of what you already have.

Is there a good time to buy and sell growth funds?

I always think that it's easier to know when to buy than to know when to sell when it comes to mutual funds or stocks. Knowing when to sell is the hardest thing to master. They're not set in stone, but these guidelines might help you decide.

A Good Time to Buy:

Your research indicates the fund's assets are undervalued

You won't need the money for at least 10 years

You are looking for diversification and professional management in your investments

A Bad Time to Buy:

Right before the fund has a capital gains or income distribution (if the money is outside of a retirement account) *and* you do not think the fund's value will increase more than the net tax amount of that distribution

You need your money within two years

You want to keep your money 100 percent safe and sound

A Good Time to Sell:

There has been a fundamental change in the fund's investment style which affects your portfolio strategy

Your fund has underperformed its competitors for the past couple of years

An important portfolio manager leaves

A Bad Time to Sell:

There's a big redemption fee or deferred sales charge and you haven't given the fund a chance to perform. (A deferred sales charge is the fee attached to B-share funds that a brokerage firm deducts from your account over time, rather than up front.)

Portfolio Rebalancing

What is portfolio rebalancing?

Portfolio rebalancing refers to the adjustment of your mutual funds so that you don't have too much money invested in any one thing. What if you've invested in three or four mutual funds that invest primarily in blue-chip stocks? Your funds are doing fantastically. The market is soaring into record territory, and you have made enormous gains on your initial investment. Still, something is nagging you, and it's this: You are very pleased by how well your money is doing, but at the same time you know deep down that every silver lining has a cloud. You worry that one word from the Fed might send the markets tumbling, thus potentially wiping out all your paper profits. So what do you do? You change around the mix of your funds by selling off shares in one fund and reinvesting that money in another fund. You may keep one of your funds invested in the stock market, but for your peace of mind, you think it might be a very good idea to begin investing in T-bills. You are looking for an investment balance that you feel comfortable with and that you can live with. And sometimes that means rebalancing or changing your current fund distribution.

If I do decide to rebalance my portfolio, what do I need to be careful of?

Taxes, taxes, taxes. Remember that anytime you cash out of an investment and there are profits involved, you will have to pay capital gains taxes or ordinary income taxes (depending on your holding period) on those profits.

How often should I consider rebalancing my mutual funds?
It depends on what kind of investor you are and what has happened in the markets since you invested your money. Let's say that you had $100,000 to invest and you wanted to put 70 percent in the market and keep 30 percent safe and sound. So you put $70,000 in good no-load growth funds and $30,000 in Treasury notes. The market skyrocketed, and two years later you have a total of $165,000, $135,000 in the market and $30,000 in Treasury notes. You will see that you have closer to 82 percent of your investment money in the market and 18 percent that is safe. And you are two years closer to retirement. Now may be the time to rebalance your portfolio to put it back in line with your investment goals and guidelines.

How do I rebalance my portfolio?
If you wanted to keep that 70/30 split, you would take all of the money you had to invest—in the above example, $165,000—and put 70 percent of that (or $115,500) in the market. You would put the remaining 30 percent (or $49,500) in a safe place, such as Treasuries.

SYSTEMATIC WITHDRAWAL

I want to stay invested in the stock market, but I need money to live on. Is there a way to get money out of my growth fund on a monthly basis?
Yes. What you are referring to is known as a systematic withdrawal.

Can you explain systematic withdrawal?

Systematic withdrawal is an option for people like you whose assets are invested in mutual funds. You want to leave your money in the funds for growth, yet you need money to live on. In this arrangement, your mutual fund company redeems a certain amount of your shares every month and sends, or wires, you the full amount. History shows us that stocks grow at a rate of around 11 percent every year, averaged over time, and most people can afford to take a percentage of that, say 4 or 5 percent, out of their mutual funds every year without depleting the principal in the fund.

What if there's a bear market?

Then you can call your mutual fund company and arrange to get less money in your systematic withdrawal. If there's a raging bull market, you can arrange to get more. It's your money, and it's up to you.

How long does a bear market last?

Well, there is no way to know for sure, for when it comes to the market, history will not necessarily repeat itself. However, in the past, bear markets normally have lasted between six months and two years, with the norm being between six and eighteen months.

Will I have to pay taxes on the amount that the mutual fund sends me every month?

It will depend on whether you have a gain over your purchase price. If you do, you will. If you don't, you won't.

Does systematic withdrawal work with all types of mutual funds, or just certain kinds?

This is a crucial question, and the answer is that systematic withdrawal works best, naturally, with a high-performing fund. I'm talking either a growth fund, or a growth-and-income fund. Since these funds typically invest in blue-chip stocks, the chances of these funds faltering are significantly lower. I would not, however, use the systematic withdrawal system to take money out of a bond fund. These funds typically don't grow very fast, so you may be unintentionally gnawing away at more of your capital than you intended. Remember, taking money out this way regardless of the fund that you are in does not guarantee that you will not be chipping away at your principal. If you need income and you cannot risk losing any of the money that is generating this income, then individual bonds would be a far better investment option, in my opinion.

Taxes, Taxes, Taxes

The following questions apply only to mutual funds held outside of retirement accounts.

What exactly will I owe taxes on with a mutual fund? First, please remember that the mutual fund taxes I'm going to discuss apply only to mutual funds held *outside* of retirement accounts. When *you* sell any shares of your mutual fund, you will have to pay taxes on whatever profit you make. If your mutual fund makes a profit, meaning the *fund* sells shares of stock at a gain, you will also have to pay capital gains taxes on whatever that profit is, even though you didn't sell any of your shares in the fund. In either case, the amount of tax will be different depending on whether the profits from your mutual fund were short-term or long-term. You also will owe taxes on dividends that the fund distributes to you or reinvests for you. You do not have to pay the IRS any taxes on income that you earned from tax-free money funds or tax-free municipal bond funds, which we'll discuss a bit later.

What is the difference between short-term and long-term profits?

Short-term profits are net profits from the sale of a stock or mutual fund that was held 12 months or less. Long-term profits are net profits from the sale of a stock or mutual fund that was held 12 months or longer.

What is the difference in the actual amount of tax that I will be charged?

If you have made long-term profits, then you will be taxed at a maximum of 20 percent. (Starting in 2001, it will be 18 percent in some cases.) If you have made any profits on a security that you or your mutual fund sold within the 12-month mark, these short-term profits will be taxed at your ordinary income tax rate, whatever that may be (currently up to 39.6 percent).

What is a capital gains distribution?

At the end of every year, all mutual funds, whether stock or bond funds, that have made gains, will distribute that gain to you in cash or allow you to use it to purchase more shares of the fund—it's up to you. In either case, this is known as an end-of-the-year capital gains distribution. What this means is that at the end of the calendar year, the fund offsets its gains against its losses, and if they still have gains, they pass those gains on to you. When they do this, you will have to pay taxes on those gains.

Why does a fund have to pay an end-of-the-year capital gains distribution?

Mutual funds are not allowed to keep the profits they have made from the sales of stocks that they own. At the end of the year, all those profits must be distributed to their shareholders.

Am I entitled to this distribution even if I just bought into the fund?

Yes, but this is not necessarily what you want to have happen to you. You see, you get the money but you also must pay taxes on it. In addition, the fund lowers the price of its shares or NAV by the amount of the distribution. So as you can see, between taxes and a lower share price or NAV, taking an end-of-the-year distribution could cost you more than it might make you.

I still don't understand why an end-of-the-year gain is so bad.

Let's say that you just bought into a mutual fund at $45 a share at the beginning of December. The NAV of the fund has stayed right around 45 for the whole month. Now here we are at the end of December, and the fund distributes $3 per share of capital gains distribution. When they do this, they lower the price of the shares to $42 to reflect that distribution. You now will owe taxes on that $3. Let's say you are in the 30 percent combined federal and state tax bracket. You will now owe $0.90 of that $3 to the government in taxes. That leaves you with $2.10. Add that to the price of the mutual fund, and you now have a total of $44.10. But you bought the shares at $45 apiece. You now have a loss, because of the capital gains distribution! Also, if you owned a lot of shares of that mutual fund company, the distribution of short-term gains could put you in a higher tax bracket, thus costing you money in other areas of your finances as well.

If I reinvest my capital gains distribution, do I still have to pay taxes on it?

Yes. Taxes are always owed, regardless of whether or not you reinvest your dividends and/or capital gains distributions.

So you would avoid investing in a mutual fund in the month of December?

Not necessarily. Whether I invested in a managed mutual fund that was going to have a capital gains distribution in December would depend on my situation as well as on what I thought the growth potential for that mutual fund might be. Deciding if you want to buy a mutual fund before or after the distribution date has more to do with whether or not you think that particular fund could go up in value between the time you buy it and year-end by more than the amount of the taxes you will owe. For instance, let's say that a fund is going to distribute 5 percent in capital gains distributions at the end of the year. You will have to pay tax on that 5 percent distribution. Assuming that you are in a 30 percent tax bracket, 1.5 percent of that gain will be lost to taxes. So you must ask yourself if you feel that the fund will appreciate by 1.5 percent or more between now and the time that the capital gains will be distributed. If, in the above example, the fund went up in value by 10 percent between the time of purchase and the distribution, then you would miss out on an 8.5 percent after-tax gain by not investing. If the fund didn't go up in value by at least 1.5 percent, then you would take a loss and would have been better off waiting. How clear is your crystal ball?

It's impossible to say that it's *always* better to wait until the beginning of the next year to invest simply to avoid capital gains taxes. Sometimes it is and sometimes it isn't. Every situation is different and should be looked at objectively.

Please remember two things: First, end-of-the-year capital gains taxes are a potential problem only if you own funds outside of a retirement account. In a retirement account, capital gains distributions do not matter, since you do not pay taxes currently on that money anyway. Second, there are many mutual funds that do not make significant capital gains distributions.

What funds do not make capital gains distributions? Index funds, for one. Since index funds buy the whole index, they do not generally distribute large capital gains. Why? Because they buy and sell only when one of the stocks of the index is removed and replaced. Since a fund that matches the S&P 500 Index is meant to track the stocks in the index, it has to buy and sell as necessary to match the stocks in the index. But trades occur with nowhere near the frequency they do in a managed fund. So if the thought of paying taxes on unexpected capital gains worries you, this should be taken into consideration before you decide on a managed fund or an index fund.

There are also funds that are known as tax-efficient funds. The managers of these funds keep in mind that the people who are buying the funds do not want to pay end-of-the-year capital gains taxes, so the funds do not have a very high turnover ratio in their portfolios.

So if I don't want to have to deal with capital gains distributions, I should look for a low turnover ratio fund? Unfortunately, it isn't quite that easy. If you buy an index fund or a SPDR, turnover ratio will not be a problem. However, even if a fund has a low turnover ratio, it does not mean it won't have a large capital gain one day. By the late 1990s, many managed funds had in their portfolios stocks that they had held for years. Even funds that don't buy and sell stocks at a high frequency have what is known as "embedded capital gains" from long-held stocks that have to be taken into consideration. Embedded capital gains are earnings that a fund has in its stock portfolio that it has not yet cashed in or realized.

Why do embedded capital gains have to be taken into consideration?

Let's use this example to illustrate embedded capital gains: Suppose Fund A has a low turnover ratio and has owned a technology stock for two years. Now almost 20 percent of their portfolio is this one stock with a cost basis of $50 a share. (The cost basis is the original purchase price.) For one reason or another, the fund manager decides that he now wants to liquidate the entire holding of this stock, which, let's say, is currently trading at $350 a share—$300 more than the cost basis. Can you imagine the capital gains distribution that you will be hit with? If you really want to avoid capital gains taxes, SPDRs are the way to go.

Capital gains taxes don't sound so bad to me. Are they?

Well, depending on how much money you have in the fund, you may be unpleasantly surprised to see what this capital gains distribution does for you. Taxes are taxes, and what you pay out in taxes is money that's no longer growing for you. Think of it this way: All a managed mutual fund cares about it is making the greatest return for you, which makes sense from the fund's point of view. The fund doesn't care whether or not it's a convenient year for you to pay taxes on capital gains.

I received a dividend from my mutual fund this January, but on my statement it said that it was declared in December of the previous year. Do I owe taxes on this money for last year?

You absolutely do. Often a mutual fund will declare a dividend at the end of the calendar year but not pay it until January of the following year. Nevertheless, you are considered to have received the dividend in the year in which it was declared.

If I lose money in my mutual fund, can I write off the loss?
Yes, only if you sold your interest in the fund and have a realized loss, not just a paper loss. Be advised that there is a maximum for capital losses during a single year—currently $3,000—if you do not have gains to offset it.

If I sell my mutual fund, how will I know what gains (if any) to report on my income taxes?
Your mutual fund company will send you a Form 1099-DIV, Dividends and Distributions (or a substitute form containing substantially the same language), telling you what you must report or take into account on your income tax return.

I have read that capital gains distributions should be added to the cost basis of mutual funds. Does this apply if the capital gains were not reinvested in the mutual fund?
No. If the gains were not reinvested, nothing changes in regard to your holdings. However, if you reinvest your dividends and capital gains distributions into the fund, where they are used to buy additional shares of the fund, they become part of your cost basis.

I have accumulated a lot of shares in a mutual fund over the last few years, and now I want to start selling just a few of them off. What is the best way to do that, tax-wise?
I would sell off the shares that have the highest cost basis first. This will lessen your tax burden. However, not many people keep track of the dates that they purchased shares of a mutual

fund and what their cost basis, or purchase price, was at the time. Most mutual fund companies provide for you what is known as your *average cost basis,* which is the average price for all the shares that you have purchased. You can use this figure to calculate your capital gains taxes.

Bond Funds

In my opinion, mutual funds have a time and a place in most people's portfolios. The mutual funds that we were just discussing are geared mainly toward growth, and are made up, in large part, of stocks. In this section, we will discuss a kind of mutual funds suited to investors looking for income rather than growth: bond mutual funds. Let me say right now that I am not a big fan of bond funds. I believe that if one wants income, the best way to get it is via individual bonds, along with utility stocks and preferred stocks, all of which I talk about in *Ask Suze . . . About Stocks and Bonds.* But if you're considering buying bond funds, here is some information you should know.

What Is a Bond Fund?

A bond fund is simply a mutual fund that is made up entirely of bonds. A bond is simply a security issued by the government or a corporation that obligates the issuer to pay the bondholder a specified sum of money, usually at specific intervals, and to repay the principal on a certain date. Like bonds, bond funds come in all shapes and sizes. You can get a municipal bond fund, a municipal bond fund for the state you live in, a corporate bond fund, a bond fund made up entirely of Treasuries or high-yield bonds, a short-term bond fund, or an intermediate-term bond fund. The list goes on and on.

Is the interest rate for a bond fund fixed or variable?
The interest rate of a bond fund is not fixed as it is for a single bond. A bond fund's interest rate will fluctuate along with interest rates in the economy, although it will lag behind them a bit. Remember, however, that bond funds pay income every month without fail and many investors like knowing they can rely on that check even if the amount of the check may vary.

Do bond funds have maturity dates?
No, bond funds do not have maturity dates—that is, a date on which you will be paid back the face value of the bond or bonds you purchased. This lack of a maturity date leaves you in the position of never knowing for sure how much of your original investment you will get back. Now, the only way to get your money out of a bond fund is to sell your shares. Let's say that interest rates have risen since your original purchase, and, for whatever reason, you have decided to sell your shares. You will most likely *not* get back all the money you put into the fund. However, the reverse is true as well. If interest rates have declined since your original purchase, when you sell your shares you most likely will get back more than you invested. This is the risk of a bond fund: You could get back what you put in, you could get back more, or you could get back less. This risk does not exist with an individual bond since bonds have maturity dates that tell you exactly when the bond will pay you back the principal, regardless of the interest rate environment. Big difference, if you ask me.

What determines if the price of the bond fund goes up or down?
Primarily interest rates. If interest rates go up, the price of the shares of the bond fund will tend to fall. If they go down, the price of the shares of the bond fund will tend to go up.

Is that price movement guaranteed?
No. If the fund is poorly managed, the price of the fund could go down and you could lose money even if interest rates fall. In contrast, the price of individual bonds will always go up when interest rates fall, and vice versa.

I bought my bond fund when interest rates were high. Why is my income going down with interest rates?
Because when new money comes into the fund, the portfolio manager buys bonds with this money. If interest rates have dropped since you invested your money, the bonds the fund manager is buying with the new money will have a lower yield. This will affect the overall yield of the bond portfolio, which in turn affects your yield.

Do I still have to pay capital gains taxes on a bond fund?
All bond funds distribute capital gains just as growth funds do. If you are in a municipal bond fund, do not be surprised if at the end of the year, you end up with a capital gains distribution on which you have to pay income tax, even if your main objective in buying into the fund was to avoid taxes. In addition, bond funds reduce their share prices by the amount of their distributions just as growth funds do.

Characteristics and Kinds of Bond Funds

There are so many different bond funds to choose from. How do I decide which bond fund is right for me?
Before we get into this discussion, there are a few things that you should keep in mind. Although your bond fund has no

maturity date, the maturity dates of the individual bonds *in* your fund will have a big influence on your total returns. The longer the *average maturity* of the bonds in your fund, the greater the risk to you when interest rates fluctuate. The *quality* of the bonds in the portfolio also makes a big difference in regard to risk. The lower the quality of the bonds, the higher their yield, but the higher the risk as well. Because bond funds come in all sizes and shapes, you can have many different varieties of funds within a specific category. For example, you can have a Treasury bond fund with bonds that have short-term maturities or long-term maturities—each is a Treasury bond fund, but each reacts very differently to a change in interest rates. So you can see it is important to know not only what type of fund you might want to invest in but the characteristics of the fund as well. Let's look at some different characteristics and categories of bond funds, and questions that people ask about them.

Short-term Bond Funds

We'll begin with short-term bond funds. Short-term here refers to the fact that the bond fund typically owns bonds that have an average maturity date of anywhere from one to five years, and sometimes even less. This doesn't necessarily mean that this bond fund only buys short-term bonds, it's simply an overall investing philosophy. In my opinion, short-term bond funds could be a good temporary shelter for your money, since it is unlikely that they will rise and fall dramatically with interest rate fluctuations. Of course, since they are less risky than other kinds of investments, their yield will be lower. Still, they will generally out-earn what you could make in a CD or a money market fund.

INTERMEDIATE-TERM BOND FUNDS

Intermediate-term refers to bond funds made up of bonds whose average maturity date is from five to ten years. Intermediate-term bond funds can be quite a bit more volatile than short-term funds, though they are still generally considered less risky than long-term bond funds.

LONG-TERM BOND FUNDS

Long-term refers to funds that invest in bonds with a typical maturity date of anywhere from 10 to 20 years or longer. These funds usually pay the highest interest rates, but they can be extremely risky as well. Often, intermediate-term bond funds can provide investors with approximately the same total returns, with a lot less risk attached. I would not recommend long-term bond funds unless interest rates are extremely high and projected to come down. Even if this was the case, you would still be far better off, in my opinion, in long-term individual bonds.

When it comes to short-term, intermediate-term, and long-term bond funds, how do I know which kind is right for me?

For me, the answer to this question totally depends on what is happening with interest rates. If interest rates are about to go up and you still want to buy a bond fund, then I would suggest looking for one with very short-term maturities. If interest rates are relatively stable, an intermediate-term fund would be okay. And if interest rates were about to come down after a period of being very high, long-term funds would be the best choice. Remember, the longer the average maturity of the bonds within a bond fund, the more volatile the per-share price and the greater its fluctuation will be. It will move farther downward when interest rates go up, and vice versa. But, again, individual bonds of the same duration would probably accomplish your goals better than funds.

How can I find out the length of the maturities of the individual bonds in a bond fund?

Morningstar, a mutual fund rating service (*www.morningstar.com*), lists the maturities of individual bonds in bond funds.

Now that you know the different characteristics of bond funds, you need to know the different categories. Remember that each one of these bond funds can be made up of long- or short-term maturities. The five categories that you most likely will come across are Treasury bond funds, mortgage bond funds, corporate bond funds, municipal bond funds, and high-yield bond funds.

Treasury Bond Funds

A Treasury bond fund invests exclusively in U.S. Treasury bills, bonds, and notes. Most people who invest in Treasury bond funds are looking for absolute safety in terms of the quality of the bonds in the portfolio. But remember, even with Treasury bonds the price per share of your fund can fluctuate according to interest rate movements.

Mortgage Bond Funds

Mortgage bond funds are funds that invest primarily in U.S. government agency bonds. You probably have heard these kind of funds referred to as "Ginnie Mae" or GNMA funds (GNMA stands for Government National Mortgage Association). These funds are made up of bonds that are used to finance most home mortgages across the country. They pay a little more than most plain T-bond funds, and yes, there is a federal guarantee behind them.

Are there any downsides to mortgage-backed bond funds?

Yes. With mortgage-backed bond funds, you have to be on the lookout for declining interest rates, because in this situation, many homeowners often decide to refinance in order to take advantage—and pay off their entire original mortgage at once! This means that your bond fund will get a huge chunk of their principal sooner than expected. What will the fund manager do with this extra money? He or she will pay you back some of your principal. On the surface, this may seem like a good thing, but it is not necessarily. If, for example, you invested in a fund that was giving you 8.5 percent and the fund returned some of your principal at a time when new investments were paying you only 5 percent, then you would not be making that 8.5 percent on those funds that you thought you had locked in.

Corporate Bond Funds

Corporate bond funds are made up of bonds issued by corporations. They are less safe, of course, than government bond funds; however, they pay you a higher yield and in my estimation they are definitely worth looking into if you are set on buying a bond fund. Still, I have to tell you once again, individual corporate bonds are a better way to go than corporate bond funds.

How can I get the highest yield out of my corporate bond fund?

The highest-yielding bond funds are also the riskiest: You have not only interest rate risk but also the risk of the company defaulting. Many of these high-yield funds offer very attractive interest rates, and investors light up like a pinball machine when they hear they can get a 2 percent higher yield per year than they could on most other bond funds. Do you remember the junk bonds of the 1980s, and how controversial they were? (Junk bonds—also known as high-yield bonds—are bonds that have lousy credit ratings.) If the companies that issue these bonds default, investors stand a good chance of getting *nothing* back—no principal and, of course, no interest. Investing in a high-yield bond fund as opposed to a single bond means you do not risk the loss of your entire principal and interest, but even one company defaulting on its bonds can still cause the fund's share price to drop dramatically.

Please always remember that the longer the average maturity of the bonds in your fund, the higher its yield and the greater the possible risk. Add junk bonds to this mix, and you will find yourself the owner of a very high-risk, potentially high-yielding bond fund. You can buy funds containing high-yield bonds of almost any kind—municipal or corporate, for instance, which basically invest in cities, counties, or corporations that have low credit ratings. Do you really want to take this chance with your money? You might, depending on the interest rate and the corporations involved.

Insured Municipal Bond Funds

Municipal bond funds invest, of course, in various municipal bonds (often called munis for short). Municipal bonds are bonds whose interest is paid by individual cities, counties, or states. These bond funds are insured against default by two enormous private insurance companies, the American Municipal Bond Assurance Corporation and the Municipal Bond Insurance Association. These monoliths ensure that whoever is issuing the bond, whether a city, a county, or a state, is in solid economic health and at little risk of defaulting. What do insured muni bond funds offer? Tax-free interest income and the assurance of getting the majority of your principal back. (Remember, how much you get back depends on the price of your shares when you sell.)

Uninsured Municipal Bond Funds

So, whether or not a municipal bond fund is insured affects its yield. Why is this?

Because insured municipal bond funds have to pay for their insurance, and what they pay comes out of their shareholders' take. But if you invest in an uninsured municipal bond fund, there is no insurance payout. It's as simple as that. Just like insured muni bond funds, some uninsured muni bond funds try to invest in the most stable municipal bonds out there. The only difference is that no one is insuring them in the event of default.

Do all municipal bond funds escape taxation by state and federal governments?

No. In order to avoid state taxes, you must buy a municipal bond fund that invests only in municipal bonds from the state in which you are a resident.

How do I know if a municipal bond fund has my state's bonds in it?

The name of the bond fund will include your state name—as in, for example, the Vanguard California Tax-Free Fund.

If my state does not have a state income tax, should I still buy a municipal bond fund that invests only in bonds issued by my state?

No. Buy a municipal bond fund (or a municipal bond) that will give you the highest yield—keeping in mind your tolerance for risk, of course—from any state.

International Bond Funds

As their name suggests, international bond funds invest in bonds issued in foreign markets. (If your prospectus describes your bond fund as global, it includes some U.S. bonds as well.) My advice? International bond funds are not for the first-time bond fund investor! The least risky ones invest in bonds issued by foreign governments, or by stable foreign companies that focus on different industries, not just one. The riskiest international bond funds are those that invest in so-called "emerging market" countries, i.e., countries in Latin America, Asia, or Eastern Europe. The fund's prospectus will tell you exactly where the bond fund intends to put its money. Bear in mind that whenever you invest abroad, your money (and thus your yield) is subject to the fluctuations of the currency markets. This means that your international bond fund will lose money if the value of the U.S. dollar increases against foreign currencies. Also, the interest rates of other countries cannot be predicted in the same way as those in the United States.

I know of many people who have done well with the higher yields offered by international bond funds, but I also know people who have had some unpleasant surprises related to currency devaluation.

BOND FUND QUESTIONS AND ANSWERS

Why do some people prefer bond funds to individual bonds?
People often prefer bond funds to individual bonds because they offer monthly versus semiannual income. And like all mutual funds, bond funds offer diversification, which makes people feel safer.

Do bond funds have any other advantages over individual bonds?
If for some reason you need cash in a hurry, you can write checks against the amount of your principal in a bond fund. I would advise against doing this, however, since whenever you do, you are selling off shares, and you will have to pay capital gains taxes on any profits.

If I'm going to buy a bond fund, what should I keep in mind?
Here are a few tips and definitions for you to remember. First, the *current offering price* is the dollar amount that people who want to buy this fund will have to pay. Remember, all bond funds that trade as open-end mutual funds (which means that the number of shares they can sell is unlimited) are valued by an NAV, or the net asset value of the fund. Again, this is the total worth of the portfolio at the end of every day, less any liabilities, divided by the number of shares of the fund that have been issued. When you sell your shares, you will get the NAV of your fund on the day you sell it.

The current offering price of the fund I am interested in is different from its NAV. What does this mean?
This means that the fund charges a load. If it is a true no-load fund, the NAV and the current offering price will always be the same. (By the way, the price of a fund only reflects the load, if there is one, and not the fees you're charged each year once you buy into the fund.)

Do I need a portfolio manager, or can I act as my own?
If you buy individual bonds, you will in essence be your own portfolio manager, deciding which bonds to keep or sell; your broker can guide you in that process. If you buy a fund, those decisions will be made for you by a professional portfolio manager. This is the person to whom you should be more than willing to pay a management fee, because this is the person who will make you money. The management fee in a good bond fund should be half a percent, give or take a fraction. If it's more than this, you've got a greedy manager.

Please note: Every fund has charges in addition to the manager's fees. The expense ratio comprises all the fees the fund charges its investors. The expense ratio for a good bond fund should not be greater than 0.6 percent. The higher the expense ratio, the lower your yield.

If I am thinking of buying a bond fund through a broker, what should I be aware of?
The first thing I would look at is the load, or the sale commission. The only kind of bond fund I would want to see you buy would be a no-load bond fund. Again, no-load means no commission. You can buy or sell shares anytime you want, and it will not cost you a penny.

Which do you recommend—bond funds or individual bonds?

I have to tell you, in almost all circumstances, I have a hard time justifying bond funds over individual bonds—unless you are desperate and need the highest current yield you can get and yield is more important to you than knowing that you will get your principal back in full. Many investment advisers may disagree. They will say that you need a bond fund, especially if you do not have a lot of money, because individual bonds always carry a risk of defaulting. They will say that you need to protect yourself and diversify among a lot of bonds, which you cannot do if you don't have a lot of money with which to do so.

Do I really need to protect myself against bond issuers defaulting? What is the reality here?

In theory, it sounds correct to want to diversify among a lot of bonds to protect yourself. While it is true that some bonds carry the risk of defaulting, not all bonds do. Treasuries, for instance, are the safest possible investment you can make. If you have just a small sum of money you want to invest in bonds, then your investment does not have to be diversified as long as your money is absolutely safe. You could put every penny you have in a Treasury, regardless of your age, and your money would be safe from default. This may not be the wisest thing to do with respect to inflation risk or to the return, but the money would nonetheless be absolutely safe. So the reasoning that tells us the only way to be safe is to diversify by using a bond fund simply does not hold water, in my opinion.

What if I don't want to buy a Treasury? I am in the 28 percent tax bracket, and I would prefer to buy municipal bonds because I do not want to pay taxes on the interest.

We need to look at your money more closely. The taxes on an investment of $10,000 or less in a taxable bond are not going to be that great. Let's say you're in the 28 percent tax bracket, and you put $10,000 in a Treasury that earns 5 percent. Of the $500 you will earn in interest, $140 will go to the IRS in taxes, leaving you $360. If you were to put that same $10,000 in a municipal bond fund—let's say it paid you 3.5 percent—you would get $350 after taxes, less than the after-tax yield of the Treasury. With a Treasury you know you will get back all $10,000 on the maturity date. With a bond fund, you do not have that assurance, because bond funds do not have a maturity date.

Furthermore, if interest rates went up since you first purchased the bond fund, when you withdrew your money, you would not get back as much as you deposited. Also, if you bought your fund while interest rates were quite low, when you sell your bond fund you could get back less than what you deposited. (Remember, when interest rates increase, the rates on fixed income investments decrease.) The bottom line is, what you earned in interest after taxes is essentially the same between the Treasury and the municipal bond fund ($360 versus $350). The only difference is, one guarantees your investment principal, the other guarantees nothing.

Maybe you are thinking, Okay, but I have a lot more money than $10,000 to invest, and I do not want any more taxable income—so in my case wouldn't it make sense to buy a municipal bond fund? The answer is no. First of all, if you have a lot more money to invest, you can diversify by buying individual municipal bonds. Second, if you really want to avoid paying taxes, that's an even stronger reason to stay away from bond funds, with their capital gains distributions. Remember, most funds have an end-of-the-year capital gains distribution. So even if you go into a municipal bond fund with the sole intention of never having to pay taxes while you own it, you may very well find you are paying taxes at the end of the year.

Are capital gains taxes the only downside?

No. Some advisers might tell you that it is worth the management fees to have a professional manager watch over all the bonds in the portfolio and decide for you what to do. That may be true, but the fund manager's decisions may not always be just for your benefit. For instance, if the overall fund performance is not great, in order to beef up the annual return numbers, a portfolio manager may make decisions based on what is best for the track record of the fund—such as buying slightly longer-term maturities or riskier bonds—rather than what is best for the actual money in the fund. The goal of the fund is to attract new investors' money. The way all funds do this is to make sure the reported returns of the fund are as high as possible. Isn't that how you choose to buy one fund over another? You bet it is.

How else might the portfolio manager's decisions affect me negatively?

Imagine yourself in a bond fund. You put your money in when you could have had a coupon, or interest rate, of 7, 8, or maybe even 9 percent. New investors are entering the fund all the time, even as rates go down. The portfolio manager has to keep buying new bonds—whether your yield is high or low. This affects your rate of return. If you had bought individual bonds when the interest rates were high, you would be reaping the rewards, since your yield is fixed in individual bonds.

Are there any other reasons you don't like bond funds?

Another reason I prefer individual bonds to bond funds is that even though bond fund prices are supposed to go up when interest rates go down, and vice versa, this does not always happen. This makes bond funds unpredictable in spite of the fact that bonds are the most predictable investments of all. In addition, when interest rates go down, the interest rate that you are earning in a bond fund will also decline. If you are on a fixed income, this could be disastrous. When interest rates decline, which means you are getting less money monthly, and if the price of the fund does not increase or, worse, declines, then you could really be in trouble.

Also note that when you buy into a bond fund, you pay the current offering price of the fund on the day you place your order. You can tell your broker how much you want to spend, but you will not know for sure until the fund closes for that day how many shares you will actually get, since the NAV and the current offering price are calculated at the end of the day's trading. Or you can tell your broker how many shares you want to buy, but the actual dollar amount you've spent will not be calculated until the close of business that day. So if you place your order in the morning, when everything is just great, and then the market experiences a day of wild swings, you could end paying more than you thought per share or getting less when it translates into the yield of the fund. With a bond fund, you really have no idea what you will end up with at the end of the day. With an actual bond, you do.

Could you please sum up why it's better to buy individual bonds—with or without a financial adviser helping me?

Yes. These are the upsides of buying individual bonds: You know precisely the amount of money that you will get back at maturity date. You will never have to pay end-of-the-year capital gains taxes. You will not have to worry about the portfolio manager leaving. Nor will you have to worry about inside fees and expenses of the fund. If interest rates go down or up, you will most likely see an honest movement to the upside or downside. You will know your exact coupon rate and it will never change, even if interest rates go down. Finally, you will know the exact price that you are paying per bond and the yield that you will be getting.

If individual bonds are better for all these reasons, why does anybody buy into bond funds?
Because there are exceptions to everything—and that holds true for bond funds as well. Sometimes bond funds can be a good place to put money short-term or even intermediate-term, but for the long haul, when you are looking for a stable income and want control over your money, I would go with individual bonds. Make sure they have a safe rating, or stick with Treasuries.

MONEY MARKET FUNDS

A money market fund is simply a mutual fund that invests in liquid, safe investments, such as short-term Treasuries. Money market funds offer investors access to their money along with higher interest rates than available from passbook or checking accounts—and, in many cases, at a cost far less than the monthly expense of a checking account. Consider the fact that most savings accounts today pay about 2 percent interest. Consider, too, all the hidden charges of banking—service charges for your checking account, fees for ATM withdrawals, and so on. Then ask yourself if a money market fund is the right kind of account for you to have. I'd be willing to bet that it is.

What is the ideal use of a money market fund?

A money market fund is best used as a parking place for money that you want to be safe and sound and/or that you know you will need within the next two years.

What questions should I ask myself before I open a money market fund?

Here are a few: Is money that you want to keep liquid, safe, and sound currently earning only 2 or 3 percent in interest? Don't you wish it could be earning more? Are you paying $10 a month for check-writing privileges and not earning any interest on the money in your checking account? If the answer to these questions is yes, then you need to ask yourself: What am I doing for my money? What you can do right now is to start checking out money market funds.

TYPES OF MONEY MARKET FUNDS

There are essentially three different kinds of money market funds. These are: general purpose money market funds; government-only money market funds; and tax-free money market funds.

- General purpose money market funds invest primarily in short-term instruments and generally provide their investors with the highest yields.
- U.S. government-only money market funds play it very safe by investing in Treasury bills and government instruments. Remember, the great thing about Treasury

bills is that they are guaranteed by the U.S. government. And the nicest part of investing in government-only money market funds is that investors don't have to pay state tax on any interest income.

- Tax-free money market funds, as their name suggests, also provide investors with a tax break. With this type of money market fund, investors are not required to pay any federal taxes on their interest income.

Why are money market accounts so low-risk?

Money market funds typically invest in very short-term instruments of debt. By this I mean CDs, government notes, and T-bills with very short maturities—usually of 90 days. The best thing about money market funds is their near-guarantee that whatever money you put in, you will be able to get back out at any time, without penalty.

What do you mean by "near-guarantee"?

The net asset value of a money market fund remains a constant $1 a share—only the interest rates go up and down. Although money market accounts are not FDIC-insured, there have been very few times that the value of shares in a money market fund has dropped below $1 (and in those instances, the funds made good on the loss).

What are some advantages of investing in a money market fund?

Easy. Again, since money market funds invest primarily in short-term debt instruments, any risk due to changing interest rates is significantly lowered. Plus, the rules for diversifying money market funds are far more rigorous than the rules governing diversified mutual funds that invest in stocks. Do you remember how for a regular mutual fund no more than 25 percent of a fund's assets can be put in a single investment? With money market funds, the rule is no more than 5 percent. This ensures that if one or another investment starts to do poorly, the rest of the fund will not be seriously affected. Also, if a money market fund invests in commercial paper—that is, corporate debt—a very high percentage of that debt instrument (almost 95 percent) has to be rated A1 by Standard & Poor's or Moody's. (See *Ask Suze . . . About Stocks and Bonds* for an explanation of these ratings sources.) And if a money market fund has invested in a debt instrument that carries a variable rate, the fund manager must ensure that initial rate is solid enough that if it wobbles it won't affect the overall value of the fund. As you can see, money market funds are designed to minimize risk and to provide you with protection from jiggly markets.

FINDING THE RIGHT MONEY MARKET FUND

I've decided that I want to invest in a money market fund. How do I start looking for a good one?

I am glad that you said "invest" in a money market fund, since it is important to remember that you are *investing* your money. As with any kind of mutual fund, I would first read the fund's prospectus and any annual or quarterly reports you can lay your hands on. Some of these can be downloaded right off the Internet. Second, I would check to see what kinds of debt instruments the money market fund invests in. The least risky (and probably the lowest yields) would be if the fund invested in Treasury securities. You could probably find a higher yield (and a slightly higher risk) with a money market fund that invested in Eurodollars or commercial paper, i.e., corporate debt.

To find the money market funds paying the best interest rates, check a financial magazine such as *Kiplinger's*, *Money*, or

Smart Money. Every month they list the best-performing money market funds in the United States, along with their telephone numbers. I feel, too, that you can never go wrong with getting yourself a Schwab One money market fund at Charles Schwab, a major discount brokerage firm with locations throughout the country. (In fact, that is where my mom and I have our money market accounts.) If you have $25,000 or more that you want to keep liquid, safe, and sound, Charles Schwab has a money market account called the Value Advantage, which pays about one-half of a percent more than other Schwab money market accounts.

Anything else I should be on the lookout for?
As always, read the fine print. Find out if there is a minimum amount you have to write a check for in case you need your money in a hurry. Does the fund offer wire or electronic transfers so you can get your money sooner rather than later? Is there a charge for writing a check or for withdrawing some of your money? Keep these things in mind.

Making the Most of a Money Market Fund Account

How much cash do I need to open a money market fund account?
You can usually open one with as little as $500 to $1000.

You said that my money is always available to me. Does this mean I have check-writing privileges?
Generally, yes, you do.

Then why shouldn't I just transfer all the money in my checking account into my money market account? That

way I can earn higher interest but still have check-writing privileges!

Be careful. A money market fund is *not* the same as a checking account. I don't blame you for getting confused, because money market accounts do closely resemble bank accounts. Most money market accounts will permit you to write checks against your account balance, but many institutions set a limit on the number of checks you can write every month. And some money market funds stipulate that the checks you write have to be in amounts of $300 or greater, though others do not. Ask about this before setting up your account.

How else is a money market fund account different from my regular bank account?

Bank accounts are insured by FDIC; money market funds are not. But money market funds generally pay higher interest rates and cost you far less in fees.

My bank offers a money market fund to its depositors. Does this mean that if I open a money market fund account at my local bank branch my money will not be insured?

Here's an exception to what I said above. Very recently, banks have begun to offer money market funds in order to compete with the mutual fund companies. These accounts are insured by the FDIC, but their yield tends to be a lot lower, because of the high cost of the banks' overhead.

I have a money market fund with about $30,000 in it. Is there any danger in this?

Not with regard to the safety of your money, but a risk of having more than $5,000 or $10,000 in a money market account is that it is possible—probable, in fact—that someone representing the bank or brokerage firm where the money is kept will call you, offering to help you invest this money for a better rate of return. (Many banks now have in-house brokerage services to help their clients invest.) Obviously, the bank or brokerage firm will make more money in the long run if you invest this money in certain ways rather than others. So these companies keep an eye on accounts with a consistent stash of cash, in the hope that if they call you, you will be open to listening to their ideas. Please be careful if this happens. Don't do anything you don't want to do. It's your money. Just keep in mind, and say so, that your goal with these funds is to keep them safe and sound and available in case of an emergency.

Certificates of Deposit (CDs)

Certificates of deposit, or CDs, are a type of savings instrument issued by a bank or a credit union (or even a broker). Like individual bonds, they pay you a specified rate of interest over a preset period of time, and pay back your principal at maturity.

Are CDs insured by the Fed?

CDs are insured up to $100,000. Anything over this ceiling will not be insured by the Fed. Granted, banks don't make a habit of going belly-up, but you want to cover your assets in a worst-case scenario, so keep that $100,000 limit in mind.

When should one invest in a CD?

Like money market funds, CDs are a very safe, very conservative part of an investment portfolio. I think CDs are a very good place to park savings you might be holding for an expense you anticipate in the near term, and I also think CDs are a good place to put funds for a short period of time until you decide what you are going to do with them on a long-term basis. But I would not recommend keeping the lion's share of your money in CDs, unless it is the only place where you feel your money is safe and sound and you need current income.

Shopping for CDs

Should I buy a CD from the bank where I keep my checking and savings accounts, or is it worth my while to shop around?

I would certainly inquire at your bank whether or not the fact that you are already a customer affects the rate of the CD (and also if opening a CD may lower your banking fees)! Sometimes banks favor their long-term customers and customers with larger combined balances. If the answer is no, then I would shop around for the best rate.

What is the most important thing for me to keep in mind as I shop for a CD?

The first thing I would want to know is what the CD's maturity is. The next thing to find out is the current interest rate.

Will I be penalized if I take my money out before the maturity date?

Yes. You will usually be charged an early withdrawal penalty, or EWP. Check with the bank offering the CD to find out how much this penalty is, as it varies.

Does every single bank in this country penalize customers if they withdraw their money early from a CD?

The majority of them do, but more and more I am seeing banks that have waived the EWP. This waiver has a price, however: lower interest rates. So you have to ask yourself whether or not it's worth it. Better yet, decide beforehand, to the best of your knowledge, if you might need this money before the maturity date. None of us can predict the future or those times when life will throw us a curveball. But you can certainly prepare for uncertainty—for example, by buying CDs in smaller denominations and/or staggering their maturity dates.

How does buying smaller denominations and/or staggering maturity dates prepare me for uncertainty?

Well, given that most banks *will* charge you an early withdrawal penalty, you can minimize the amount on which you might have to pay this penalty. If you invested $80,000 in a CD and for some reason you decided to take your money out early because you needed just $10,000, the bank would charge you an EWP on all $80,000. Wouldn't it have been just as easy—and in the end, cheaper—to have bought eight certificates of deposit at $10,000 apiece? This way, if you need emergency money and want to cash out one of your CDs, the bank will levy an EWP on a CD of only $10,000. And if your CDs have different maturity dates, at least some of your money will be available to you more frequently—perhaps when you need it—instead of all at the same time.

What else should I ask banks when I am looking for a CD?

Another question I would ask the bank is about variable-rate CDs. Depending on the interest-rate climate, these may offer higher or lower returns than a fixed-rate CD. If you think that interest rates are bound to rise in the near future, then you should definitely think about putting your money in a variable-rate CD, which allows you to take advantage of rising rates and protects you, by its withdrawal features, in case rates fall or you need access to your funds. I've already mentioned the advantages of staggering your maturity dates. This means that you have one CD that comes to maturity in six months, another that comes to maturity in a year, etc. This acts as a partial protection against interest rate fluctuations.

Most importantly, find out about the rate of return (the annual percentage yield, or APY). Interest rates are dependent on the maturity of the CD, and they also vary from bank to bank. Finally, you should also ask how often interest is paid or credited to your CD. Is it daily? Monthly? Quarterly? The more often it is credited to your account, the better, of course, for you.

Would I ever want to buy a CD through my broker?

Actually, I recommend buying CDs through a broker. Yes, you read that right! Some CDs that are bought through your broker have one big advantage that CDs that are bought from a bank do not have: They can be sold (and bought) on the secondary market. Let's say you bought a five-year CD, and six months into it you need your money. Rather than taking an automatic interest rate hit or an EWP, you can instruct your broker to sell your CD for you on the secondary market. If interest rates have fallen since you purchased your CD, you could get back more than you invested. (This is because another investor may be willing to pay a premium for the higher interest rate attached to your CD.) If they have stayed the same, you could get back what you put in; if they have risen, you could get back less. But in any case, you will probably come out better than you would at the bank. And a brokerage firm can shop the whole country for you to find you the best rate or a buyer, if necessary. So check it out, for this may be one time a broker is worth consulting.

What is an "odd-term" CD?
An odd-term CD is a kind of CD with an unconventional time period until maturity—for example, 5 months or 17 months—as opposed to the standard 6-month maturity.

What is a "step-up" CD?
A step-up CD allows you to lock into the current interest rate and take advantage of rising rates during the term of the CD—usually between one and five years—by converting to the higher yield without penalty. Most banks will allow you to step up to a higher rate once during the term of the CD, but you must notify the bank to initiate the step-up process; it does not automatically occur once rates change.

Do you think buying a Treasury note is better than buying a CD? If so, why?
There are plusses and minuses to both CDs and Treasury notes. Treasury notes pay you interest that is not taxed at the local or state level. Any interest that you make on your CD is taxable at the local, state, and federal levels. So the bottom line depends on your tax bracket and the interest-rate difference. Overall, I prefer Treasuries to CDs because of the tax advantages and government guarantees. Also, you can invest far more than $100,000 in a Treasury note and still have your money be safe and sound.

ANNUITIES

An annuity (regardless of kind) is a contract, or policy, between you, the policyholder, and an insurance company, which invests on your behalf. The minimum investment in most annuities is usually around $5,000. While that money is invested in the contract, you do not owe taxes on any interest or gains. You can buy an annuity directly from the insurance company, or, as with Treasury bills, municipal bonds, and corporate bonds, through a brokerage firm, a discount-brokerage firm, a bank, or a mutual fund company. There are many different kinds of annuities offered today.

Why would anybody want to buy an annuity?

Tax deferral. In my opinion, annuities are an investment instrument that is way oversold so brokers can make big commissions. However, some annuities these days are an excellent means of deferring taxes on money that otherwise might be invested in CDs or Treasuries. And if you are not going to need your money or the income from it till you are at least 59½ or older, then a kind of an annuity known as an SPDA can be a great investment.

Are there any risks commonly associated with annuities?

Annuities are not federally insured. This is because an insurance company, not a bank, is involved. If for some reason the insurance company from which you bought your annuity flounders or goes belly-up, the amount that you put into your annuity and any growth can be frozen for a very long time and/or reduced in value.

How exactly do annuities work?

This is a complicated question to answer because there are many different kinds of annuities—different not only in how they invest your money but also in how they are taxed. Let's start with the components shared by every annuity.

The Owner

You. The person who purchases the contract, or policy, is know as the *owner,* or *policyholder.* (Two people or more can own a policy, as co-owners). As the owner, you can make any changes (of beneficiary, of the amount of the distribution) you want, anytime you want—you own the policy, after all. You can also name a successor owner, someone you designate to step in as owner of the policy in the event of your death or, in some cases, incapacity.

The Annuitant

In order for an annuity to qualify as a legitimate insurance contract—which is what allows it to enjoy tax deferral—someone has to be insured. This person is known as the *annuitant.* The annuitant has no power whatsoever over the money—unless, as is often the case, the owner and the annuitant are the same person. You can be your own annuitant. When you choose to annuitize your policy, or receive monthly income from this investment, the annuitant is the recipient of those payments, for the rest of his or her life. The *amount* of the payments, which are usually made monthly, is determined by the annuitant's age. For example, if I bought an annuity and named my mom as the annuitant, she would qualify for much more money each month than I would if I were the annuitant. This is because the monthly payments are based on the annuitant's life expectancy. The older the annuitant, the shorter their life expectancy, and the shorter the amount of time the insurance company will have to make those monthly payments, and so the larger each payment will be. While we are on this subject, you should also know that if the annuitant is female, her payment amounts will be different than if the annuitant is male. Why? Because according to the actuarial tables that insurance companies use, females are expected to live 5 to 10 years longer than men.

The Beneficiary

The beneficiary is the person or people to whom you, as owner, will leave any money remaining in the annuity when you die. The owner decides how much to leave each beneficiary. The beneficiary and the annuitant cannot be the same person, but the owner and the beneficiary can. For instance, I could own the policy, have my mother be the annuitant, and name myself as beneficiary. More commonly, however, the owner and the annuitant are the same person, and a different person, or persons, is named the beneficiary.

Buying an Annuity

How do I buy an annuity?
You can buy an annuity in one of several different ways. You can buy one through a lump-sum payment, in which you pay the entire sum all at once, or you can buy an annuity by making monthly or annual payments to the insurance company. If you buy the annuity all at once, then it is called a single-premium annuity.

What if I buy an annuity, but the next day, God forbid, I get hit by a truck?
It will depend on the contract you signed, but in most cases the insurance company will pay the beneficiary named on your policy the face value of your contract, plus interest, if there is any.

Do annuities have to go through probate for my beneficiaries to get my money?

No. If you name a beneficiary who survives you, your annuity will avoid probate. If, however, you name your estate as beneficiary, the annuity will probably have to go through probate.

How do I choose an insurance company that's right for me?

I would start by looking at how the insurance company I am interested in purchasing an annuity from is rated by the following insurance-rating services.

The only acceptable ratings are:

AM Best—A or better
Moody's—Aa or better
Standard & Poor's—AA or better
Duff & Phelps—AA or better

The insurance company can tell you what their ratings are, or you can call the ratings companies directly and ask them. The insurance company will also give you literature documenting their ratings.

If I like their ratings, what else should I look for?

Before you consider taking out an annuity, you should request information from the insurance company in question. You should pay very close attention to the renewal interest rates that the company has given policyholders in years past. If, for instance, you are buying an annuity with a good interest rate for the first year, do you know what the insurance company will pay you the second year, the third year, and so on? How long is the interest rate guaranteed for and how do they decide how to renew it?

How else can I tell how good, or how bad, the insurance company I'm considering is?
Here are a few more things to bear in mind when you are shopping for an insurance company. Just as with mutual funds, you should take a look at the quality of the investments held by the insurance company. In *Ask Suze . . About Stocks and Bonds,* I talk about junk bonds, or bonds that have a rating of BB or lower. If you find that junk bonds make up more than 10 percent of your insurance company's total invested holdings, you should be wary. I would also be very interested in finding out whether your insurance company pays regular dividends. If it has begun withholding dividends, this can be a sign that the company is strapped for cash.

How do I find out all this information? Presumably the insurance company itself won't volunteer it.
Actually, the insurance company will provide this information if you just ask them. Most of them will be very honest with you and should be able to show you this information in writing.

Tax Laws, Penalties, and Annuities

Are there any tax laws that I need to know about in regard to my annuity?
In most circumstances you cannot withdraw any earnings of your annuity prior to the age of 59½ without incurring a 10 percent penalty tax. So for the privilege of tax deferral on these funds you forfeit free access to your money until you reach the age of 59½. There are exceptions to this if you buy an imme-

diate annuity or if you annuitize the annuity that you have, but as you read on, neither of these options is a great investment opportunity for you.

If I am already past age 59½ and I put money into an annuity, will the insurance company let me take it out anytime I want without penalty?

No. Even though the federal penalty tax does not apply to you, there is still a penalty imposed by the insurance company. Most annuities have what is known as a surrender period, a set amount of time—usually 5 to 10 years—during which you have to keep the majority of your money in the contract to avoid a penalty. Most contracts will allow you to withdraw at least 10 percent of the accumulated value of the account a year without a surrender charge, even during the surrender period. If you take out more than that 10 percent, you will have to pay a surrender charge on the amount that you have withdrawn in excess of 10 percent. That surrender charge usually starts at around 7 percent of the amount of the withdrawal and drops to zero by the time the surrender period is up.

I'm getting a little confused here. Can you give me an example, using actual numbers?

Sure. Let's say you are 60 years of age and put $50,000 into a nonqualified annuity that is paying you an annual return of 5 percent for the next 5 years. At the end of the third year, your annuity is worth $57,881. You need $7,000. You can withdraw 10 percent of the $57,881, or $5,788, without any penalty whatsoever. The additional $1,212 you need will cost you approximately $60, based on a surrender charge of 5 percent. And you will owe ordinary income tax on the whole $7,000.

Please note that if you were 40 rather than 60 years old and needed $7,000, you would have to pay the IRS the 10 percent early withdrawal penalty—or $700—plus ordinary income tax on that money.

Qualified Versus Nonqualified Annuities

What's the difference between a qualified and a nonqualified annuity?

If you are investing with money that you have already paid taxes on, then you will be buying what's known as a nonqualified annuity. If you're investing with pretax money, then you will be buying what's known as a qualified annuity. Usually this happens when you buy an annuity within your IRA or retirement plan at work, or when you transfer your 401(k) or 403(b) retirement plans into an annuity.

How exactly does the IRS tax me?

Nonqualified annuities (see below) that have been purchased after August 13, 1982, are taxed on a LIFO method, which means last in, first out. Any interest or gains that your fund has earned are considered to have been put into your account last, and therefore, this is the money that has to come out first—and it is treated as taxable income. Once you have withdrawn your earnings, then you can withdraw your original deposit without incurring any additional taxes. If you happen to die with money in a nonqualified annuity, your beneficiaries will have to pay income taxes on any earnings when they withdraw those funds. With a qualified annuity, since you have never paid taxes on this money, all of it is taxable when you (or your beneficiaries) take it out.

Do I pay annual income tax on undistributed earnings on annuities?
No. Remember, this is one of the good things about annuities—in fact, one of their main selling points. Whatever your annuity earns is considered tax-deferred until the money is withdrawn. Your initial investment tends to grow quicker, since not only your principal but also your tax money earns interest. But remember: If you withdraw money before age 59½, you will be taxed the 10 percent early withdrawal fee by the IRS, added to which is the surrender charge of 5 to 7 percent levied by the insurance company.

Deferred Annuities

What is a single-premium deferred annuity?
A single-premium deferred annuity, or SPDA, is an annuity that you buy with a single premium. You get a guaranteed interest rate for a specific period of time, one year or more. The taxes on the interest you earn are deferred until you make a withdrawal.

Who would want to buy an SPDA?
Anyone who wants to let his or her money grow risk-free while deferring income taxes, with the main goal being income later in life. Many people enjoy the idea of a fixed interest rate that will remain in effect for a specified period of time, from one to seven years. In most cases, the longer the guarantee, the lower the interest rate. This type of annuity is most easily compared to a certificate of deposit at a bank. In both cases, you get a guaranteed interest rate for a prescribed period. In an annuity, you incur surrender charges if you take your money out, and in a CD you'll be faced with a three- to six-month early with-

drawal penalty if you withdraw money before the time period is up. The difference, however, is that with a certificate of deposit, you will be paying taxes each year on the interest you have, even if you don't withdraw it. With the SPDA, you will not pay taxes until you make a withdrawal.

Immediate Annuities

An immediate annuity, also known as an SPIA, or single-premium immediate annuity, is a contract with an insurance company that guarantees the annuitant a fixed income beginning as soon as the investment is made and continuing for the rest of his or her life, and, in some cases, continuing—to the beneficiary—for a certain period after the annuitant's death. For this promise, however, you must sign over all the money you have deposited in the annuity to the insurance company with full knowledge that you will never be able to touch it again, apart from receiving the monthly income.

Are there any tax advantages to an immediate annuity?
Yes. Part of each monthly payment is considered a return of principal, so that portion of your payment is not taxed. The return of some of your principal in addition to the interest your funds are earning enables the company to pay you a higher monthly income than you could probably get elsewhere on a guaranteed basis.

What is that monthly amount of an SPIA based on?
The amount of interest you will receive is based on your age, current interest rates, and the maximum amount of time you have chosen for the company to pay out that stream of in-

come, even if you were to die. The income options range from the highest monthly amounts of life only, to lower amounts known as life plus five or ten years certain.

LIFE ONLY

If you were to choose *life only*, the insurance company would pay you a certain amount of money every month, starting immediately, for the rest of your life. These fixed payments would continue like clockwork for as long as you are alive, even if you were to live another hundred years. You cannot outlive the income stream of an annuity, no matter what option you choose.

If, however, you opted for life only and you died the month after you had started to receive this income, well, too bad—the payments stop, and your beneficiaries get nothing. The reason that this option gives you the highest monthly income is that the insurance company knows that once you die, they're off the hook.

How does this insurance company decide how much it's going to pay you each month?

Your monthly payout—known as your income per thousand—is determined by a number of factors, including your age, your medical history, and the current interest rate environment. An insurance company can usually project your life expectancy with a pretty fair amount of accuracy, though their methods of calculation are somewhat mysterious the older you get. And different insurance companies can offer you different rates, so it's worth your while to do some research.

I don't understand the term income per thousand. Can you elaborate?

Yes. I will use an example. Let's say that you are a 70-year-old man and you enter into a life annuity. Based on its experience and its trusty tables, the insurance company will assign you a certain amount of money per thousand dollars that you have invested in the annuity. Let's say that you have purchased an annuity that is worth $100,000, using a single premium. And let's say that the insurance company has agreed to pay you the grand sum of $9.42 per thousand dollars, for the rest of your life. This means that starting every month after you have paid your premium, the insurance company will pay you $942.00.

Can you give me an idea of what the current life expectancies are?
Sure. According to the American Council of Life Insurance, if you are a man aged 60, you are expected to live another 18 years. If you are a woman, you are expected to live another 23 years. If you are a man aged 65, you are expected to live another 14 years; a woman the same age is expected to live 19 more years. At age 70, a man is expected to live another 12 years, and a woman is expected to live another 16 years. If you are a man who has made it to age 75, you are expected to live another 9 years. At age 75, a woman is expected to live another 12 years.

What happens if the insurance company is wrong and you die sooner than they have projected?
Then the insurance company wins big time. If you live to your full life expectancy, then they are within the limit of their projected calculations. If you live far longer than expected—well, they figure that doesn't happen very often, so it's not a financial disaster for them.

What if I fool the insurance company, take good care of myself, and live to be 100 years old?
Then you will get the last laugh, and I congratulate you heartily. You win big, and the insurance company loses big.

Using the above figures, the insurance company is paying you $11,304 every year. Remember, you bought your annuity when you were 70 years old. You die when you are 100. Can you figure out how much the insurance company has paid you over those 30 years? I can—it comes to $339,120.

So you are basically saying that I should get a life annuity only if I can be pretty sure that I can outlive the company's life expectancy tables?

Actually, I am not. In reality, there is no way of knowing how long we are going to live. Our death may have nothing to do with our health—for example, we could die in an accident. So predicting life expectancy is simply impossible. And particularly, if you are leaving behind a spouse, children, or any other beneficiaries, I would avoid this type of annuity like the plague. Many insurance companies, however, offer another kind of annuity for people who are attracted to the life annuity but are put off by the idea of potentially losing all their capital. This is known as the cash refund annuity. Like the life annuity, the cash refund annuity will pay you an income for the rest of your natural life, again using the same life expectancy tables that most insurance companies employ. The difference is that if you die before the entire amount of your premium has been paid back to you, then the insurance company has to give your survivors the balance in a single, or lump, sum. This can be a good option for people who require a certain amount of income per month, but who are also responsible for a spouse, children, or other heirs.

There is a variation on the cash refund annuity, known as the installment refund. This basically does what the cash refund annuity does, but rather than giving back the balance in one lump sum, the insurance company continues to pay out a monthly income until the annuity is completely exhausted. There is a life plus five or ten years certain option as well.

Life Plus Five or Ten Years Certain

With this option, the insurance company will pay you your designated amount every month for as long as you live, with one big difference: If you die, the annuity will continue to pay your beneficiaries for five or ten years (your choice) from the contract date. In other words, they pay for the duration of your life, regardless of how long that may be, but for no less than a period of five or ten years from the starting date if you are not alive.

What happens if I die the second after I sign up for a life-plus-ten annuity? Does the annuity get canceled?
No. Your beneficiaries would get the income for the next 10 years. If you were to die three years after you started receiving the monthly income, the company would have to keep paying your beneficiaries the same monthly amount for seven more years. This kind of annuity guarantees you or your beneficiaries income for at least 10 years or for as long as you live, whichever is longer.

Is there any way to renegotiate during the course of my life how much income I will be getting?
No. Once you have chosen an option and started receiving your income, the amount remains the same for the rest of your life and/or for the rest of the time your beneficiaries would receive the income as well. Even if interest rates skyrocket, your fixed income is just that—fixed. This annuity contract is one that can most easily be compared with a monthly pension from a corporation.

How do I know if an SPIA is right for me?

Are you looking for a guaranteed monthly income with some tax benefits? Are you without any beneficiaries? Are you someone who immediately needs a higher income than a straight interest-bearing investment can provide? Can you afford to give up access to the principal paid for the annuity? Do you want to take advantage of a high-interest-rate environment? Then an SPIA may be right for you. The perfect time to have purchased an immediate annuity, for example, with respect to interest rates, would have been in the 1980s, when interest rates were high.

Do you recommend SPIAs?

No. Actually, SPIAs are my least favorite of all annuities. Purchasing an SPIA, especially in a low-interest-rate environment, is not something I recommend. If interest rates go up, you are stuck at the lower rate for the rest of your life. In this case, the "rate guarantee" tends to work in favor of the insurance company, not you.

Is there another way I can get monthly income from an annuity without taking an SPIA or annuitizing my annuity?

The process that we are talking about—receiving monthly income from an annuity—is known as annuitization, or annuitizing your annuity. I want you to realize that you do not have to buy an immediate annuity in order to get monthly income from an annuity. You can do so by simply withdrawing money each and every month from an SPDA, for instance. This way you are not locked into an interest rate and can have access to your money as well as leave it to your beneficiaries.

Variable Annuities

With mutual funds gaining such ground in the recent past, receiving billions of investors' dollars, insurance companies naturally wanted to get into the act. So they created what they call a variable annuity. A variable annuity is also a contract with an insurance company for a specific period of time, but when you deposit money into a variable annuity, you choose among various mutual funds within the insurance contract to invest your money. A variable annuity can have many funds for you to choose from, or just a few, depending on the insurance company. You can buy or sell these funds at any time without incurring any taxes until you withdraw the funds. At that time, your gains would be taxed as ordinary income.

How is a variable annuity different from an SPDA?

When you buy an SPDA, your money is deposited in the insurance company's general account. This account represents the assets of the company, and the company's financial experts decide the best way to invest that money. But when you purchase a variable annuity, your money is placed into what is known in insurance company slang as a "separate account." You are the person who gets to decide which funds you want to invest in. Though you have invested your money with an insurance company, you are the person responsible for tracking the fund.

What if I don't know which funds to choose?

Because insurance companies found themselves dealing with so many investors who either lacked the experience to do their own investing, or couldn't take the time to do the research, they set up what are called asset allocation funds. This is basically a mutual fund that spreads its risk among securities, bonds, and other short-term and intermediate-term debt instruments. Like a regular mutual fund, this asset allocation fund is run by a fund manager. And as with many mutual funds you can transfer your money into another fund within the same family of funds.

Are there any advantages to a variable annuity?

One of the main draws of a variable annuity is that you enjoy tax deferral. Even if you buy and sell a different mutual fund within a variable annuity every day, you will not have to pay taxes on your gains until you actually withdraw money from the annuity. This is a great benefit of the variable annuity, especially if you've had large gains in a mutual fund not held in a variable annuity that you wanted to sell but haven't because you'd have to pay so much in capital gains taxes. If you had invested in the same mutual fund within a variable annuity, you could sell it and not pay taxes until you withdrew money. When you do withdraw, however, those funds will be taxed as ordinary income.

Another advantage is that even if you invest 100 percent of your money in a risky mutual fund within a variable annuity, you are guaranteed never to get back less than you originally deposited or the current value of the account, whichever is greater. In a regular mutual fund, there is no such guarantee. But hold your horses! This so-called benefit is not free. Later we'll discuss the downside of variable annuities, which you should keep in mind before you do anything.

How do I know if a variable annuity is right for me?

Are you somebody who likes to buy and sell mutual funds often? Are you someone who is in a very high tax bracket now but plans to be in a much lower tax bracket at retirement? Then a variable annuity may be right for you.

Within a variable annuity, are there safe places to park my money?

Yes. What you first should know is that many variable annuities have a fixed portion as part of their portfolio, so you can simply change into that fund.

What if I don't like the insurance company I'm with? Can I change?

The IRS actually permits what is known as a 1035 exchange between annuity companies. That allows you to defer taxes as well. You should bear in mind, however, that you may have to pay a surrender charge if you shift annuity companies, and that often the surrender charge will be deducted before you transfer your money to a different policy. This reduces the amount of money that you have available for reinvestment.

So a variable annuity that's not in an IRA is a great way to invest in the market and not have to worry about taxes every time you buy and sell?

On the surface that is true; however, in my opinion, a variable annuity will not save you taxes in the long run, which defeats the purpose for most people who buy annuities. With a variable annuity, it is true that every time you buy or sell a mutual fund within the annuity, you do not pay taxes. It is also true that if the mutual funds you are invested in through the variable annuity pay a distribution at the end of the year (known as a capital gains distribution), you do not pay taxes on those distributions until they are paid from the annuity. However, this is where the advantages end and the disadvantages begin.

Tell me about the tax disadvantages of a variable annuity.

In a variable annuity, you pay taxes when you withdraw your money. At what rate? Your withdrawal is subject to ordinary income taxes (up to 39.6 percent). If you had held your money in the same mutual fund for more than 12 months or more outside of an annuity, you would have to pay only the capital gains rate—up to 20 percent.

Okay, you say, no big deal. You plan to leave the money to your kids and never take it out of the annuity. But you've now passed the tax problem down to your kids, because when they take the money out of the variable annuity, they will have to pay income taxes at ordinary income tax rates on any of the growth of your funds (which could be considerable), plus the additional fees and the state premium tax, if applicable. If you had simply purchased mutual funds directly and left them to your kids via your will or trust, they would receive what is called a step-up in cost basis on the value of those funds, based on the funds' worth the day you died. If they then sold those funds before there was a further upward swing, they would not owe a penny in taxes.

Can you give me an example of this in action?

You put $25,000 into a variable annuity, and by the time you die, your money has grown to $125,000. Your kids inherit the money and withdraw it. They will owe income taxes on the $100,000 gain, along with any additional fees and state premium taxes, if applicable.

Let's say you put that same $25,000 into some great tax-fficient mutual funds, and when you die, your kids inherit the money and withdraw it. If it was worth $125,000 on the day of your death, then $125,000 is their new cost basis for tax purposes. So if they were to turn around and sell this investment for $125,000, they would not owe one penny in income taxes, since they did not realize any gain. This step-up in cost basis applies to inherited investments such as mutual funds, real estate, and stocks—but not to annuities, traditional IRAs, and retirement plans.

Do you think it's better to buy mutual funds outside of a variable annuity and give up the advantage of tax deferral?

Yes. The reality is that most people tend to hold on to their mutual stocks, funds, and so on for long periods of time. If you do sell and you have held your investment for at least a year, the most you are going to pay is 20 percent, the capital gains tax rate. Frankly, this is not so bad. But when you take money out of a variable annuity, you are going to pay ordinary income taxes on the amount that you withdraw. And remember that if you are under age 59½, you will pay the IRS a 10 percent penalty tax. Finally, when you do close the account, for whatever reason, a state premium tax of about 2 percent of your original deposit could also be levied by some states.

If I already own a variable annuity, and now I decide this isn't quite what I want, what do I do?

It depends on where you have put the annuity. Let's say that your annuity is inside a retirement account. Unless you have a variable annuity that is an unbelievably great performer, I would say to cash it in as soon as the surrender charges expire and buy into some solid, well-rated, no-load mutual funds. You can probably duplicate what you had in your annuity in an IRA by buying mutual funds directly. If your returns have been horrible, even if the surrender charge is still in force, you might want to take the hit in order to get a better return. Or you could simply withdraw the 10 percent you are allowed to take out without the surrender penalty and transfer those funds into a good no-load mutual fund, and do this every year until the surrender charges are up. Since the money is already sheltered within a retirement plan, you will not have to worry about tax implications.

What if my annuity is not sheltered within a retirement account of some kind?

In this situation, everything that I noted in the previous answer still applies, but you must also consider penalties for withdrawals prior to the age of 59½ and taxation on the money when withdrawn, as well as the state premium tax (if applicable) if you surrender the account altogether. Because all these pesky factors—one of the main reasons I do not like variable annuities to begin with—have to be taken into account, I would advise you to see a fee-based financial planner who has nothing to gain from giving you honest advice. Give him or her exact, detailed specifics of your situation—everything from your age, your family situation, your assets and liabilities, your tax bracket, the terms of the annuity you purchased, and how long you have owned it to your financial goals and so on. These particulars will determine the actions, if any, that should be taken with your contract.

INDEX ANNUITIES

In their struggle to keep up with mutual funds, the insurance industry introduced yet another kind of annuity in the mid 1990s, the index annuity. This product was created to compete with the wildly popular index funds, mutual funds that tracked an index such as the S&P 500. I have to admit I like the concept a lot—for the right investors, that is.

How does an index annuity work?

Like all annuities, an index annuity is a contract with an insurance company for a specific period of time. The surrender period on an index annuity is usually about seven to ten years. The index annuity tracks an index such as the Standard & Poor's 500, and your return will usually be a set percentage of what that particular index did in the corresponding index year, up to a maximum of a given percent.

Can you give me an example?

Let's say that your index annuity will give you 50 percent of what the S&P Index returns, up to a maximum return of 10 percent per year. You invest $20,000 on March 15. By March 15 of the next year, the S&P Index has increased 30 percent. According to the terms of your annuity, the insurance company has to give you 50 percent of that increase up to a maximum of 10 percent. Since 50 percent of 30 percent is 15 percent, which is 5 percent higher than the preset yearly maximum of 10 percent, you will be credited 10 percent of your original deposit, in this case $2,000. If the S&P Index had gone up only 15 percent for the year, you would be entitled to 7.5 percent on your investment (0.5 multiplied by 15 percent equals 7.5 percent).

For those who do not want to take any risks at all, the index annuity might be a good option. Here's why. If you invested $20,000 in a particular index annuity, and the index went up 10 percent, you would end up with $21,000 for that year (50 percent of 10 percent is 5 percent, or $1,000). In an index annuity, your money can only go up; it cannot go down—unlike in regular index funds, where you claim 100 percent of the upside and 100 percent of any downward swerves as well. The next year, when the market went down 20 percent, you would not participate in that downside activity, and you would still have $21,000 in your account. The index annuity does not credit you with 100 percent of the return. It is set in reserve to protect you in the event of a downturn.

Please note: This safety feature is not true for all index annuities, so please ask.

Are there any other safety features attached to index annuities?

Yes. If you invest in an index annuity and the market goes down every year, it won't matter to you, because in an index annuity, the insurance company usually guarantees that after your surrender period is over, you will get at least 110 percent of what you originally put in. If you put in $20,000, the worst-case scenario would leave you, after seven years, with $22,000, or about a 1.4 percent minimum guaranteed yearly return on your investment, no matter what happens in the market. Remember, this is the worst-case scenario. So if you are willing to give up some upside potential, you can also protect yourself totally against downside risk with an index annuity.

TAX-SHELTERED ANNUITIES (TSAs)

Last but not least is the tax-sheltered annuity, or TSA, that many schoolteachers and hospital workers are offered in their retirement plans. The TSA really falls more into the category of a retirement plan, since money is invested in a TSA on a monthly basis, unlike other annuities, into which the principal is deposited as a lump sum. Also, all the money in a TSA is qualified money, or money that has not yet had taxes paid on it. The TSA is, in most cases, a fine investment. If you have a TSA in your retirement account, just make sure that the funds are performing in a satisfactory way.

Do you think it's a good idea to own annuities other than TSAs within a retirement account?

I'm glad you asked this question, because holding an annuity within a retirement account is a concept I have never agreed with. What sense does it make to hold a tax-shelter vehicle like an annuity in an already tax-sheltered account like an IRA? Not a lot. Are there exceptions to this? Yes. Apart from a TSA, the only two reasons to purchase an annuity in a retirement plan are these:

- You are under the age of 59½, you need access to the funds in your traditional IRA, and you do not want to pay the 10 percent early withdrawal penalty. By purchasing an immediate annuity within your traditional IRA to get monthly income, you can avoid that 10 percent penalty tax.
- You are approaching retirement age and you want to invest in the market but are afraid of losing money. You are willing to take a smaller profit if you are guaranteed never to lose a penny. Since the index annuity accomplishes this goal, even if it is within your IRA, it can still make sense.

SUMMING UP ANNUITIES

Is there ever a time when an annuity does make sense?
We have seen when TSAs and sometimes index annuities make sense. There is one other circumstance in which I would tell you to go ahead and purchase an annuity, and it's this: If your goal is to have income during your retirement years, you do not want to take any market risk with this money, you want to avoid paying taxes now but are not in a high enough tax bracket for municipal bonds to make sense, and last, you feel that you will be in an even lower tax bracket when you retire, then a single-premium deferred annuity is a great investment, regardless of your age.

I already own an annuity, and after what you've said, I wonder if I should. Any advice?
Yes. If you already own an annuity, please don't panic. Your particular situation might be precisely right for owning an annuity, and/or your particular annuity might be performing fabulously. I myself have put clients' funds in annuities—inside and outside of their retirement accounts. Why? Because it made perfect sense in their personal situations. Never automatically assume you're in a terrible investment until you've thoroughly checked it out with a trusted professional.

I hope that in these pages you have learned not only about the advantages and disadvantages of mutual funds and annuities, but also, as I said at the beginning of this book, a little more about yourself. Remember, the choice of investments you make, and the care you take with those investments once you have committed to them, says a great deal about the sort of person you are. To some degree, you and your investments are one, and I hope that you will treat your money with the same care that you would give yourself. After all, taking care of your money *is* taking care of yourself. That is why you must make financial decisions that not only will give you peace of mind and allow you to sleep comfortably at night, but that will also give your money the opportunity to flourish and grow as you may never have thought possible.

Additional Resources

Mutual Funds

Barron's (weekly)
Dow Jones & Company, Inc.
200 Burnett Road
Chicopee, MA 01020
(800) 975-8255

The "Quarterly Mutual Fund Record" provides 10-year statistics: net asset value per share; 12-month dividends from income; and capital gains distributions (these figures appear in the February, May, August, and November issues).

Business Week (weekly)
P.O. Box 421
Highstown, NJ 08520
(800) 635-1200

The annual mutual funds issue examines the best-performing funds (this usually appears in February).

CDA Mutual Fund Report
CDA Investment Technologies, Inc.
1355 Piccard Drive, Suite 220
Rockville, MD 20850
(800) 232-6362

This statistical service presents risk-adjusted return figures on all mutual funds listed in the financial media, including statistics on fund performances during various periods and market cycles.

CDA/Wiesenberger Mutual Funds Update (monthly)
CDA Investment Technologies, Inc.
1355 Piccard Drive, Suite 220
Rockville, MD 20850
(800) 232-6362

This publication provides detailed performance review and analysis of mutual funds, money market funds, and closed-end funds. The subscription price includes the annual *Panorama*, a guide and directory to mutual funds, including 10 years of performance data.

Directory of Mutual Funds
Investment Company Institute
1600 M Street, NW, Suite 600
Washington, D.C. 20036
(202) 326-5800

This directory provides a listing of some 3,000 mutual funds, both load and no-load.

Kiplinger's Personal Finance Magazine (monthly)
1729 H Street, NW, Suite 600
Washington, D.C. 20036
(800) 544-0155

A special fall issue typically contains detailed mutual fund statistics and rankings.

Forbes (bi-monthly)
Forbes, Inc.
60 Fifth Avenue
New York, NY 10011
(800) 888-9896

The August or September issue provides statistics and ratings of mutual funds.

The Handbook for No-Load Fund Investors (annual)
The No-Load Fund Investor, Inc.
P.O. Box 318
Irvington, NY 10533
(914) 693-7420

This handbook provides a solid explanation of how to invest in mutual funds, including tables of mutual fund performance and a directory of no-load and closed-end funds.

The Individual Investor's Guide to No-Load Mutual Funds
American Association of Individual Investors
625 North Michigan Avenue, Suite 1900
Chicago, IL 60611
(312) 280-0170

All AAII members receive a comprehensive book that includes a detailed analysis of no-load mutual funds, including their historical performance, statistical summaries, fund objectives and services, the name of the portfolio manager, fund addresses and telephone numbers, as well as strategies for winning mutual fund investing. (Please note: The no-load guide is published annually, in May. It is free to members, $19 for each additional member copy; the non-member price is $24.95.)

Money Magazine (monthly)
P.O. Box 60001
Tampa, FL 33660
(800) 633-9970

A special issue that appears early in the year provides mutual fund rankings by category.

Morningstar Mutual Funds
Morningstar, Inc.
53 West Jackson Boulevard, Suite 460
Chicago, IL 60604
(800) 735-0700
www.morningstar.com

Published every other week, and similar to the Value Line stock reports, this invaluable service delivers reports on individual mutual funds.

Mutual Funds Almanac
IBC/Donahue Inc.
290 Eliot Street
Box 91004
Ashland, MA 01721
(800) 343-5413

The *Mutual Funds Almanac* includes 10-year performance figures, fund objectives, sales charges, minimum investment, redemption fees, year organized, and yield.

Mutual Fund Distributions
Internal Revenue Service
Publication #564
(800) 829-3676

This IRS publication explains in detail the tax implications for mutual fund ownership.

Mutual Fund Fact Book (annual)
Investment Company Institute
1600 M Street, NW, Suite 600
Washington, D.C. 20036
(202) 326-5800

This book provides 10-year statistical data on some 3,000 mutual funds, broken down by investment objective.

Mutual Fund Sourcebook (annual)
Morningstar, Inc.
53 West Jackson Boulevard, Suite 460
Chicago, IL 60604
(800) 735-0700

This sourcebook provides performance and risk ratings on load and no-load mutual funds, as well as information on each fund.

Quarterly No-Load Mutual Fund Update (quarterly)
American Association of Individual Investors
625 North Michigan Avenue, Suite 1900
Chicago, IL 60611
(312) 280-1070

This update provides the fund performance of more than 600 no-load and low-load mutual funds by quarter over the last year, as well as over the most recent three- and five-year periods. In addition, the update provides the difference between a mutual fund's performance and that of an average of funds with the same objective, as well as the risk index, yield, and expense ratios. Also included are lists of top-performing funds and the performances of major indices. (Please note: This information is also available on computer disk with a menu-driven program; $24 to AAII members, $39 with computer disk; $30 to nonmembers, $50 with computer disk.)

Standard & Poor's Stock Guide (monthly)
Standard & Poor's Corporation
25 Broadway
New York, NY 10064

This comprehensive stock manual contains some mutual fund information, including net asset value, minimum initial purchase required, maximum sales charge, price record, and yield from investment income.

Other excellent sources include *The Wall Street Journal* and the *New York Times*, as well as most local newspapers, which provide daily and weekly quotes on mutual fund net asset values.

Insurance Rating Services for Annuities

A. M. Best (908) 439-2200
Duff & Phelps (312) 263-2610
Moody's (212) 553-0300
Standard & Poor's (212) 208-8000

Calculating Your Fund's Costs

One of the keys to investing in a mutual fund is figuring out the true inside costs of your fund. This is not the easiest thing to do since many of the funds are quite good at hiding that information. The site below will help you find the information you need. Also listed are many great sites to help you locate the funds you are looking for, and keep you informed if something happens in a fund you own, as well as advising you on which funds to buy and which ones to sell.

www.personalfund.com

This site provides the most extensive information on fees and the effect they will have on your fund's performance.

www.sec.gov/mfcc/mfcc-int.htm

If you use this site make sure you have the prospectus of the fund you are interested in handy.

www.financenterinc.com/products/funds.html

Have your account statements ready if you use this site.

www.smartmoney.com/si/tools/fundfees/

www.quicken.aol.com/investments/quanda/

Information on the Web

www.fundmaster.com

Request free annual reports and prospectuses of any mutual fund you are interested in from this site.

www.indexfundsonline.com

This site presents you with all the options available in index funds.

www.findafund.com

Tell this site what you're looking for in a fund and, as its name suggests, it will find a fund for you.

www.fundalarm.com

Fundalarm keeps track of what is going on in your mutual fund and sends you an alarm to bring important fund news to your attention.

www.ici.org

ICI Mutual Fund Connection is a good place to continue your education of how mutual funds work.

www.fabian.com

Fabian Investment Resources advises you on when to buy and when to sell your mutual fund.

www.icefi.com

Internet Closed-End Fund Investor tracks the performance of closed-end mutual funds, both in the United States and overseas.

www.vanguard.com

Vanguard is a great educational site on the subject of mutual funds.

INDEX

About the Author

Suze Orman is the author of the #1 *New York Times* bestsellers *The 9 Steps to Financial Freedom* and *The Courage to Be Rich* and the national bestseller *You've Earned It, Don't Lose It.* A Certified Financial Planner® professional, she directed the Suze Orman Financial Group from 1987 to 1997, served as Vice President of Investments for Prudential Bache Securities from 1983 to 1987, and from 1980 to 1983 was an account executive at Merrill Lynch. She has hosted two PBS specials, one based on *The 9 Steps to Financial Freedom* and the other on *The Courage to Be Rich,* and is currently a financial contributor to NBC News' *Today*. She lectures widely throughout the United States and has appeared on *Dateline,* CNN, and CNBC, and has made numerous appearances on *The Oprah Winfrey Show.*